THE MiGHTY

SKULLBOY ARMY

by **JACOB CHABOT**

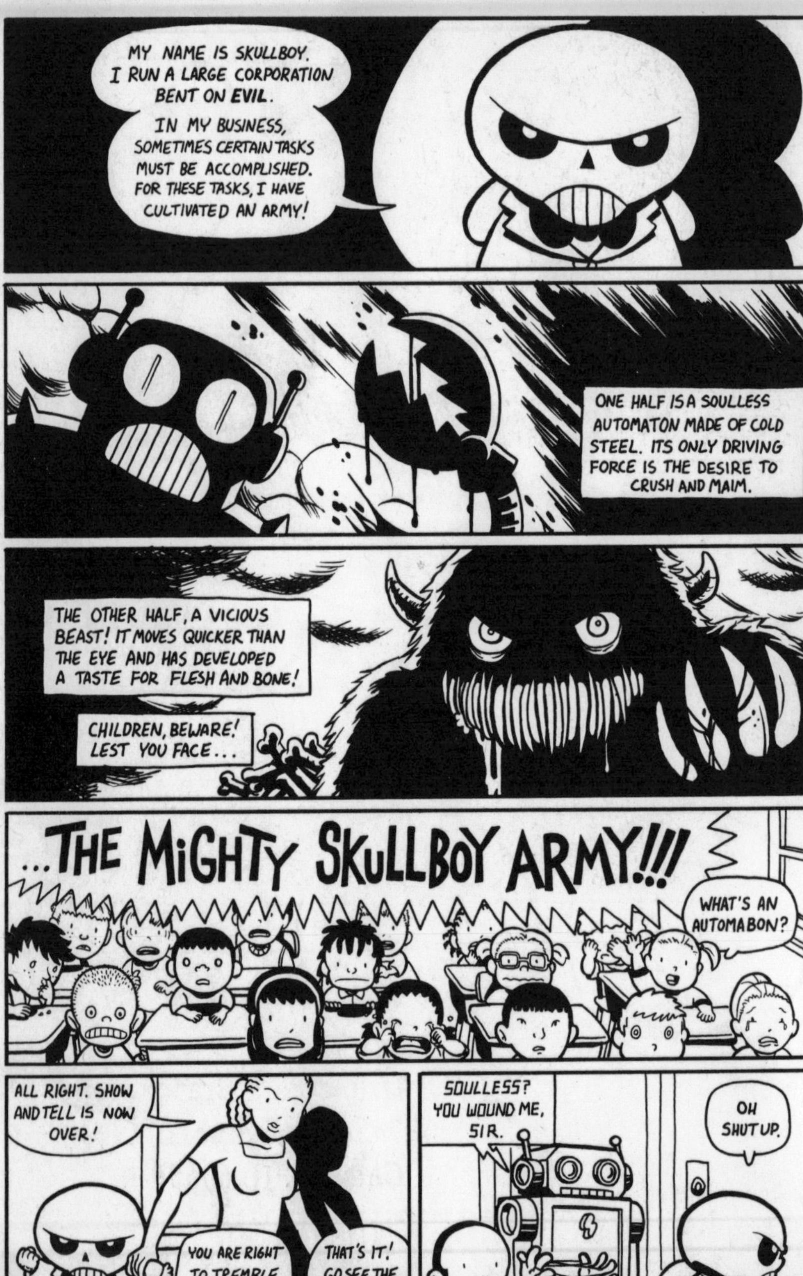
MY NAME IS SKULLBOY. I RUN A LARGE CORPORATION BENT ON EVIL.
IN MY BUSINESS, SOMETIMES CERTAIN TASKS MUST BE ACCOMPLISHED. FOR THESE TASKS, I HAVE CULTIVATED AN ARMY!
ONE HALF IS A SOULLESS AUTOMATON MADE OF COLD STEEL. ITS ONLY DRIVING FORCE IS THE DESIRE TO CRUSH AND MAIM.
THE OTHER HALF, A VICIOUS BEAST! IT MOVES QUICKER THAN THE EYE AND HAS DEVELOPED A TASTE FOR FLESH AND BONE!
CHILDREN, BEWARE! LEST YOU FACE...
...THE MIGHTY SKULLBOY ARMY!!!!
WHAT'S AN AUTOMABON?
ALL RIGHT. SHOW AND TELL IS NOW OVER!
YOU ARE RIGHT TO TREMBLE CHILDREN!
THAT'S IT! GO SEE THE PRINCIPAL.
SOULLESS? YOU WOUND ME, SIR.
OH SHUT UP.

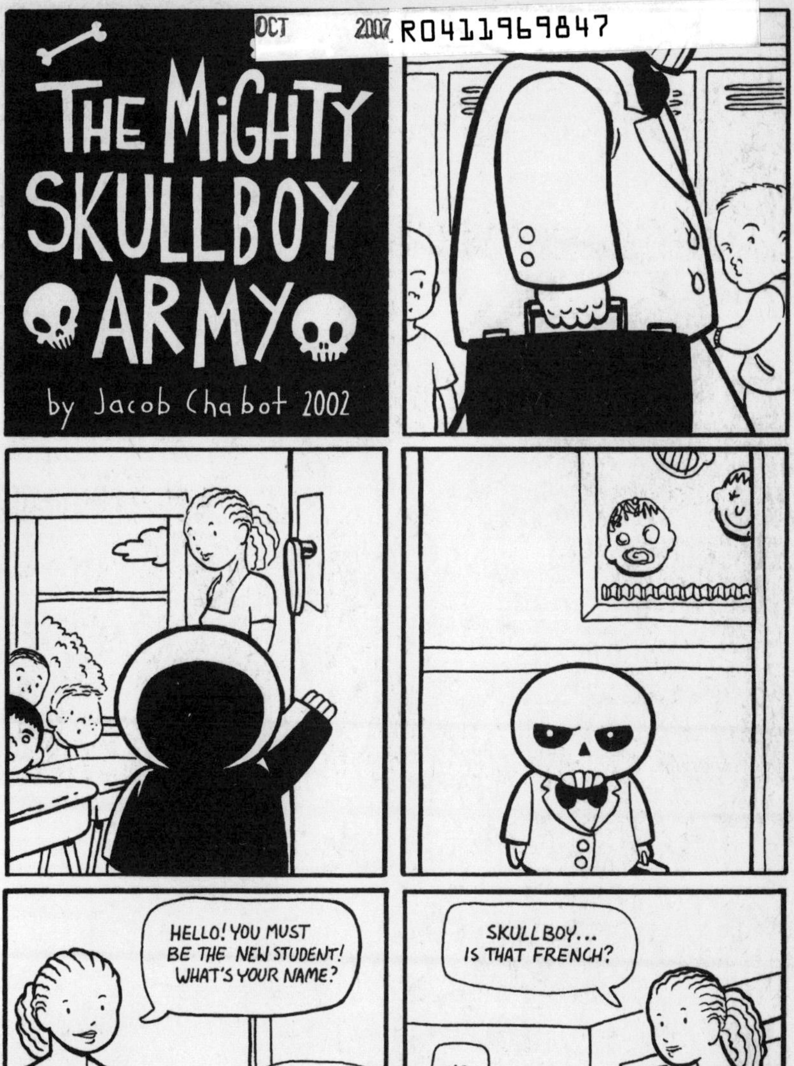
THE MIGHTY SKULLBOY ARMY
by Jacob Chabot 2002
HELLO! YOU MUST BE THE NEW STUDENT! WHAT'S YOUR NAME?
SKULLBOY.
SKULLBOY... IS THAT FRENCH?
NO.
WELCOME THEN. PLEASE TAKE YOUR SEAT.

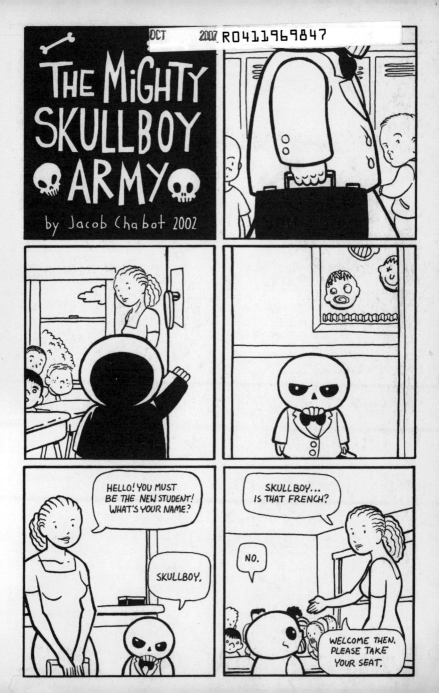

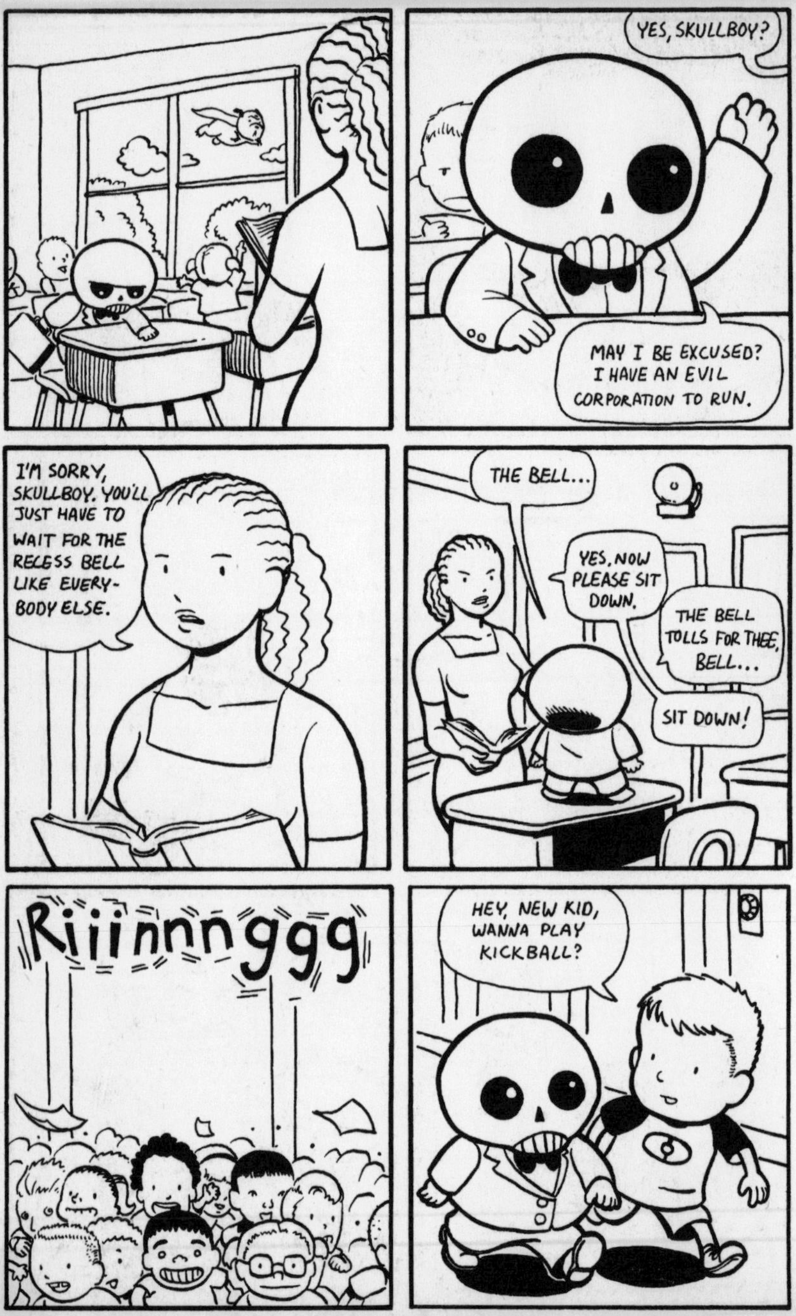
YES, SKULLBOY?
MAY I BE EXCUSED? I HAVE AN EVIL CORPORATION TO RUN.
I'M SORRY, SKULLBOY. YOU'LL JUST HAVE TO WAIT FOR THE RECESS BELL LIKE EVERY-BODY ELSE.
THE BELL...
YES, NOW PLEASE SIT DOWN.
THE BELL TOLLS FOR THEE, BELL...
SIT DOWN!
Riiinnnggg
HEY, NEW KID, WANNA PLAY KICKBALL?

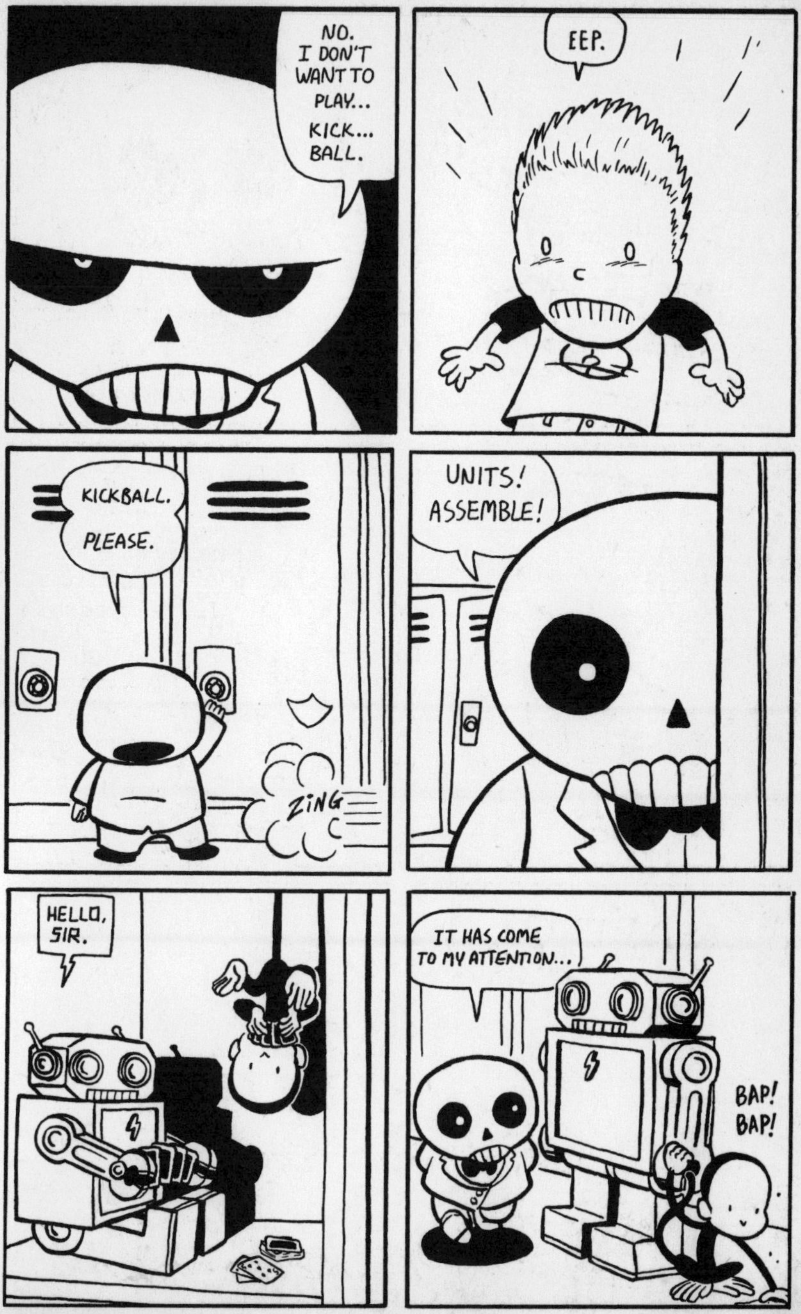
NO. I DON'T WANT TO PLAY... KICK... BALL.
EEP.
KICKBALL. PLEASE.
ZING
UNITS! ASSEMBLE!
HELLO, SIR.
IT HAS COME TO MY ATTENTION...
BAP! BAP!

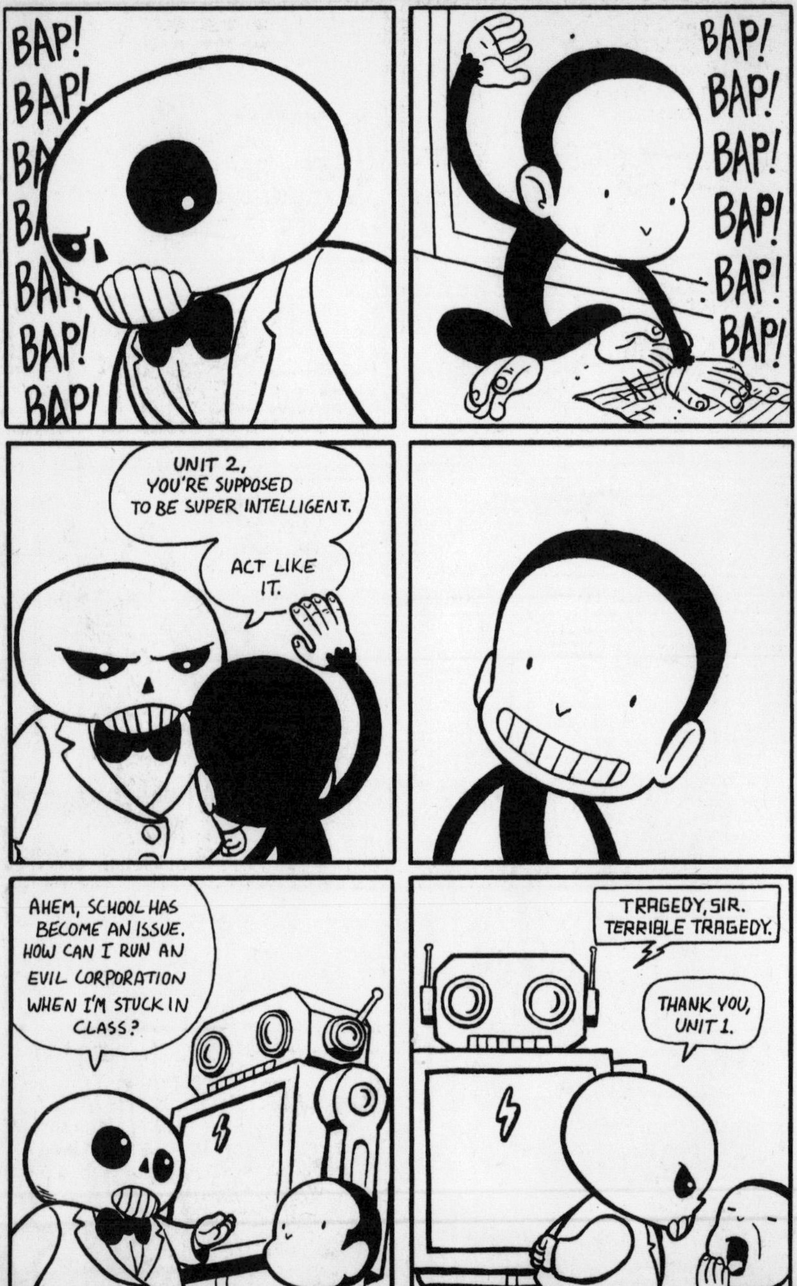
BAP! BAP! BAP! BAP! BAP! BAP! BAP!
BAP! BAP! BAP! BAP! BAP! BAP!
UNIT 2, YOU'RE SUPPOSED TO BE SUPER INTELLIGENT.
ACT LIKE IT.
AHEM, SCHOOL HAS BECOME AN ISSUE. HOW CAN I RUN AN EVIL CORPORATION WHEN I'M STUCK IN CLASS?
TRAGEDY, SIR. TERRIBLE TRAGEDY.
THANK YOU, UNIT 1.

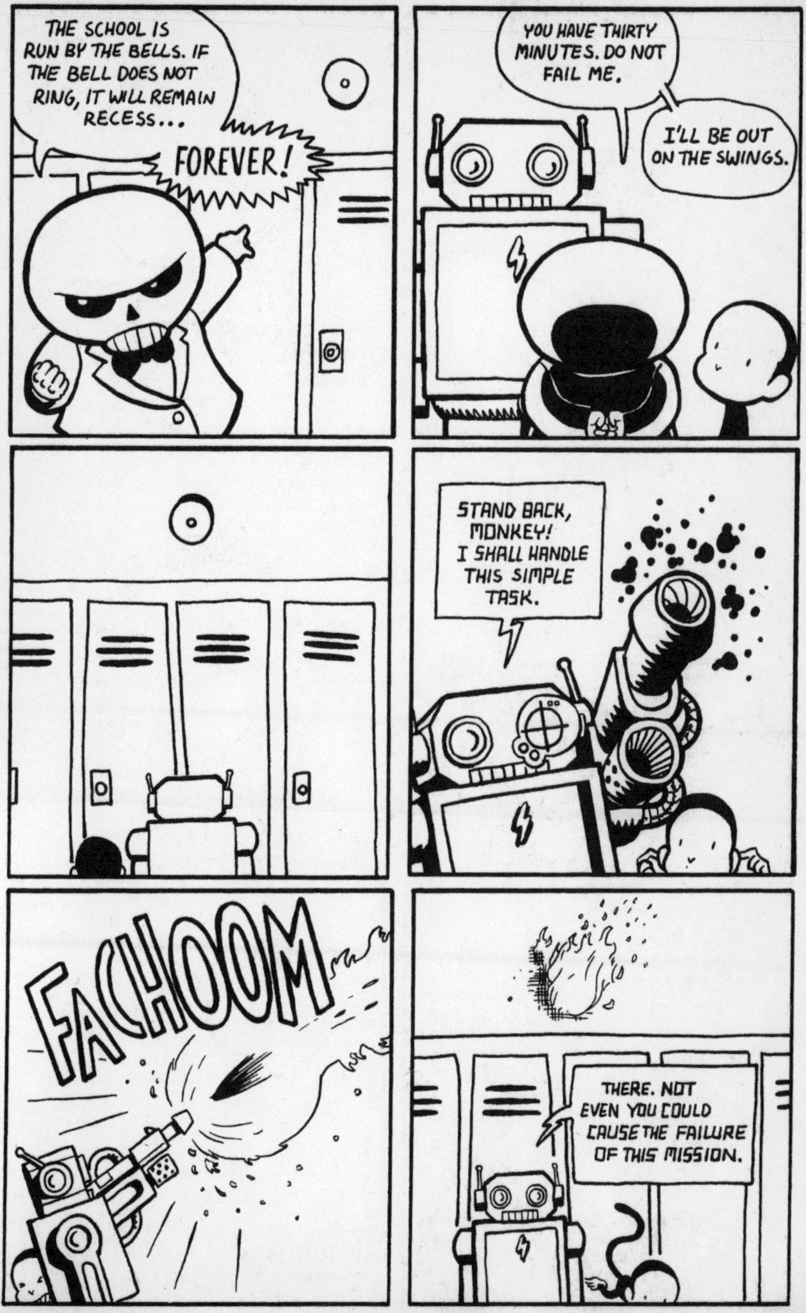
THE SCHOOL IS RUN BY THE BELLS. IF THE BELL DOES NOT RING, IT WILL REMAIN RECESS...
FOREVER!
YOU HAVE THIRTY MINUTES. DO NOT FAIL ME.
I'LL BE OUT ON THE SWINGS.
STAND BACK, MONKEY! I SHALL HANDLE THIS SIMPLE TASK.
FACHOOM
THERE. NOT EVEN YOU COULD CAUSE THE FAILURE OF THIS MISSION.

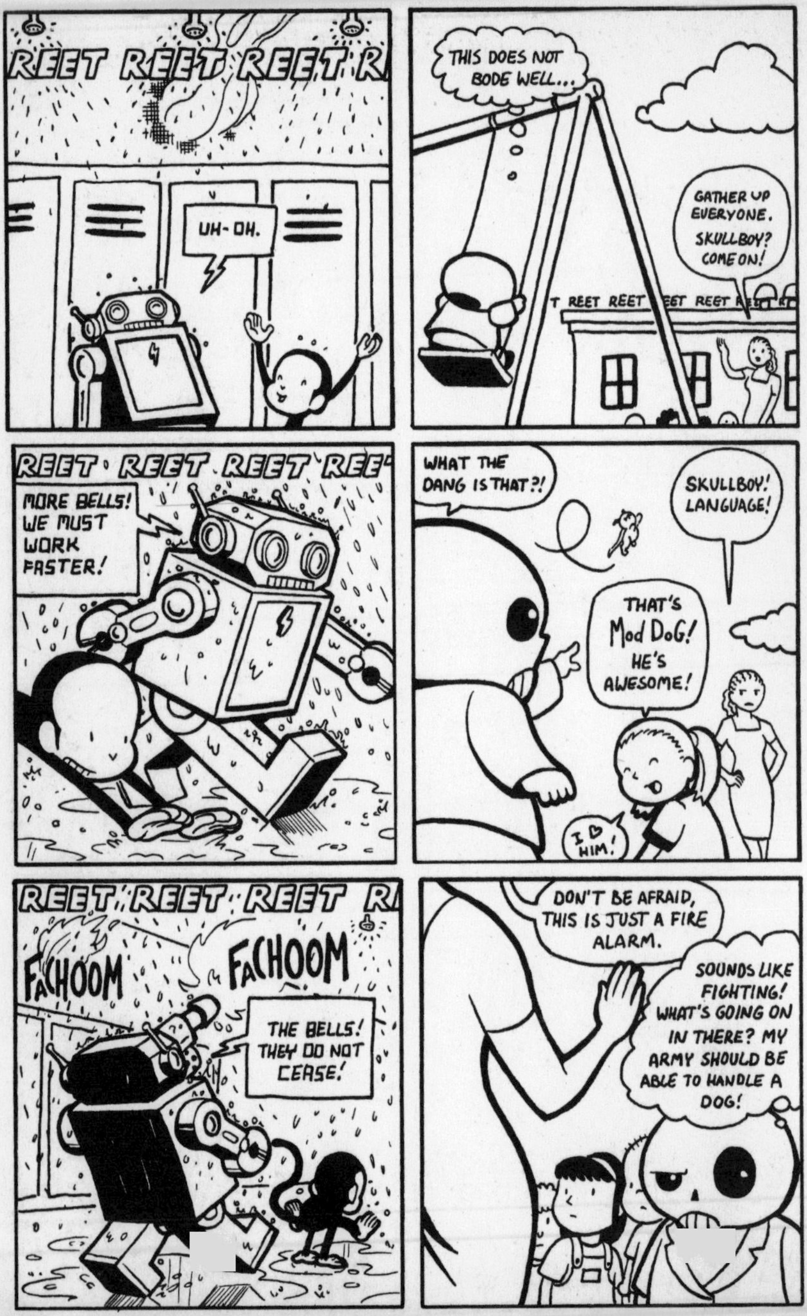
REET REET REET R
UH-OH.
THIS DOES NOT BODE WELL...
GATHER UP EVERYONE. SKULLBOY? COME ON!
T REET REET REET REET
REET REET REET REE
MORE BELLS! WE MUST WORK FASTER!
WHAT THE DANG IS THAT?!
SKULLBOY! LANGUAGE!
THAT'S Mod DoG! HE'S AWESOME!
I ♡ HIM!
REET REET REET R
FACHOOM
FACHOOM
THE BELLS! THEY DO NOT CEASE!
DON'T BE AFRAID, THIS IS JUST A FIRE ALARM.
SOUNDS LIKE FIGHTING! WHAT'S GOING ON IN THERE? MY ARMY SHOULD BE ABLE TO HANDLE A DOG!

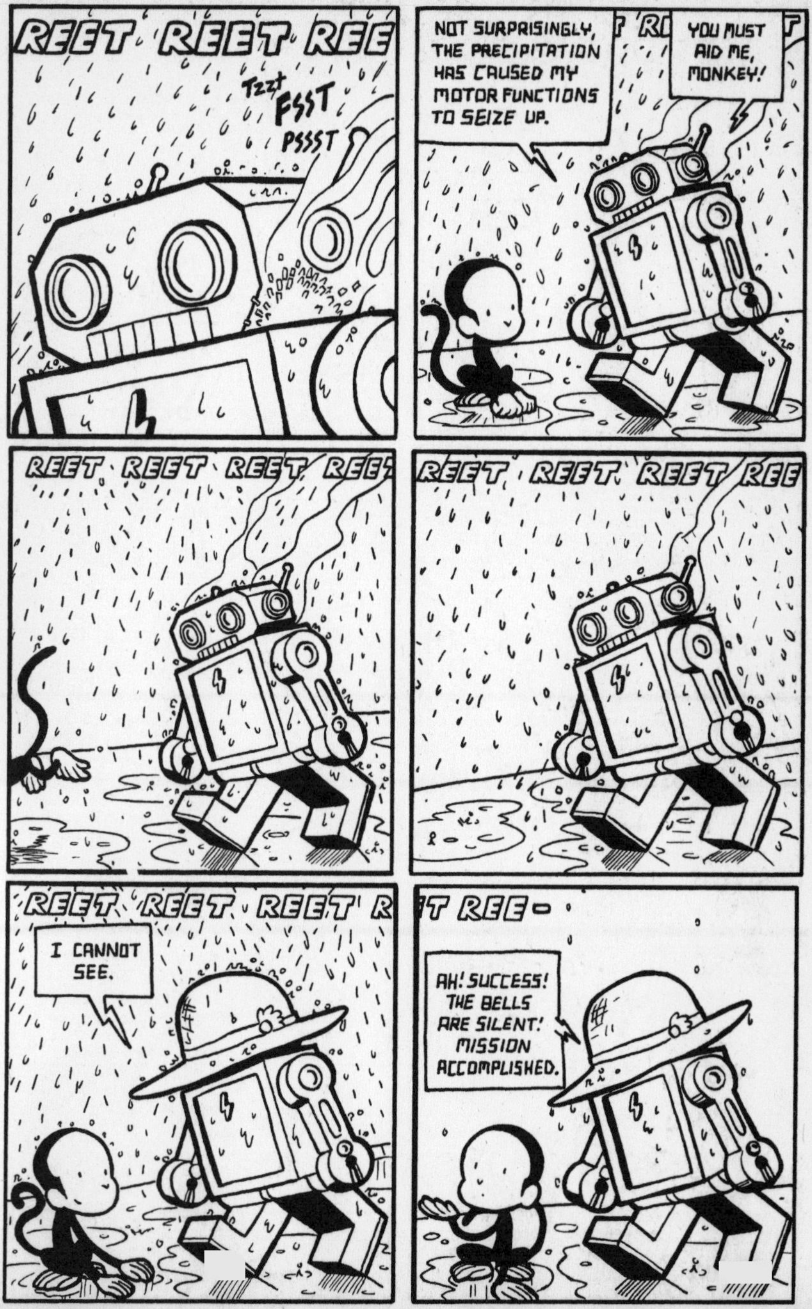
REET REET REE
Tzzt FSST
PSSST
NOT SURPRISINGLY, THE PRECIPITATION HAS CAUSED MY MOTOR FUNCTIONS TO SEIZE UP.
YOU MUST AID ME, MONKEY!
REET REET REET REE
REET REET REET REE
REET REET REET R
I CANNOT SEE.
T REE-
AH! SUCCESS! THE BELLS ARE SILENT! MISSION ACCOMPLISHED.

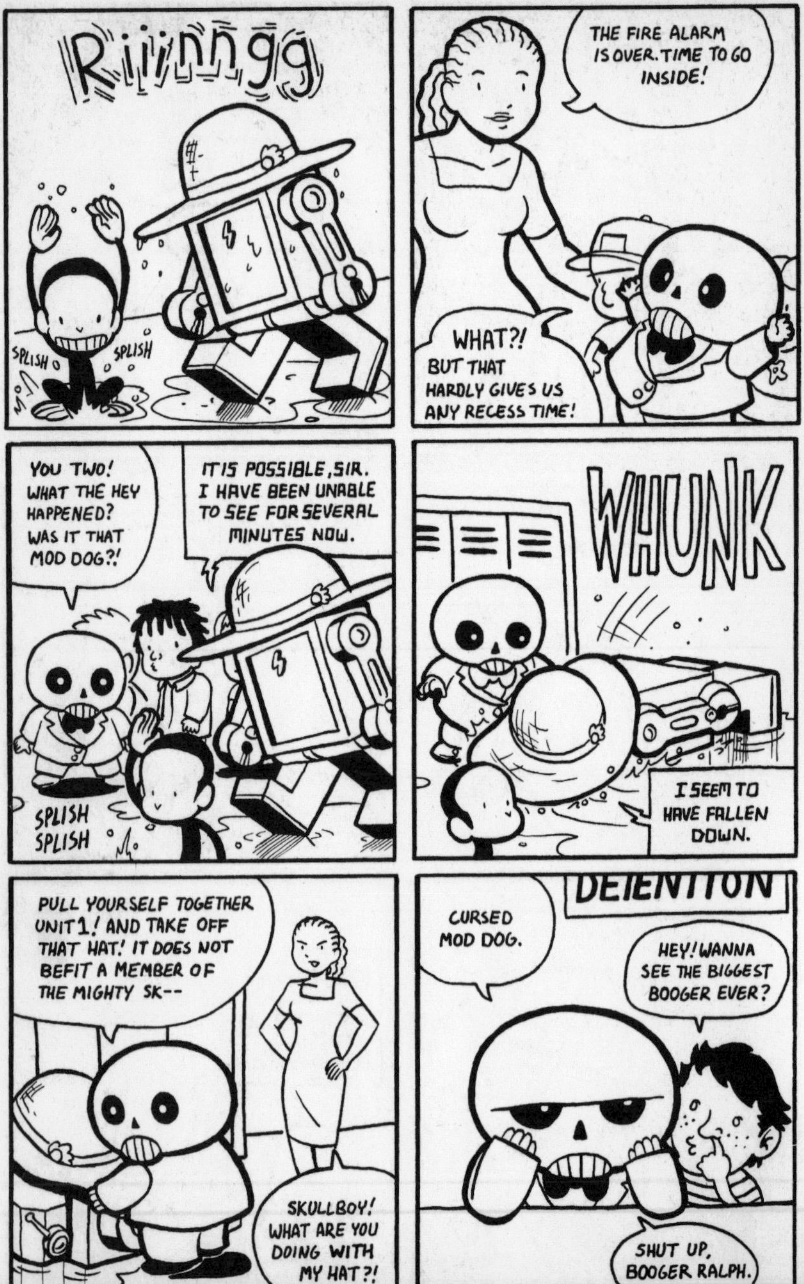
Riiinngg
SPLISH
SPLISH
THE FIRE ALARM IS OVER. TIME TO GO INSIDE!
WHAT?!
BUT THAT HARDLY GIVES US ANY RECESS TIME!
YOU TWO! WHAT THE HEY HAPPENED? WAS IT THAT MOD DOG?!
IT IS POSSIBLE, SIR. I HAVE BEEN UNABLE TO SEE FOR SEVERAL MINUTES NOW.
SPLISH
SPLISH
WHUNK
I SEEM TO HAVE FALLEN DOWN.
PULL YOURSELF TOGETHER UNIT 1! AND TAKE OFF THAT HAT! IT DOES NOT BEFIT A MEMBER OF THE MIGHTY SK--
SKULLBOY! WHAT ARE YOU DOING WITH MY HAT?!
DETENTION
CURSED MOD DOG.
HEY! WANNA SEE THE BIGGEST BOOGER EVER?
SHUT UP, BOOGER RALPH.

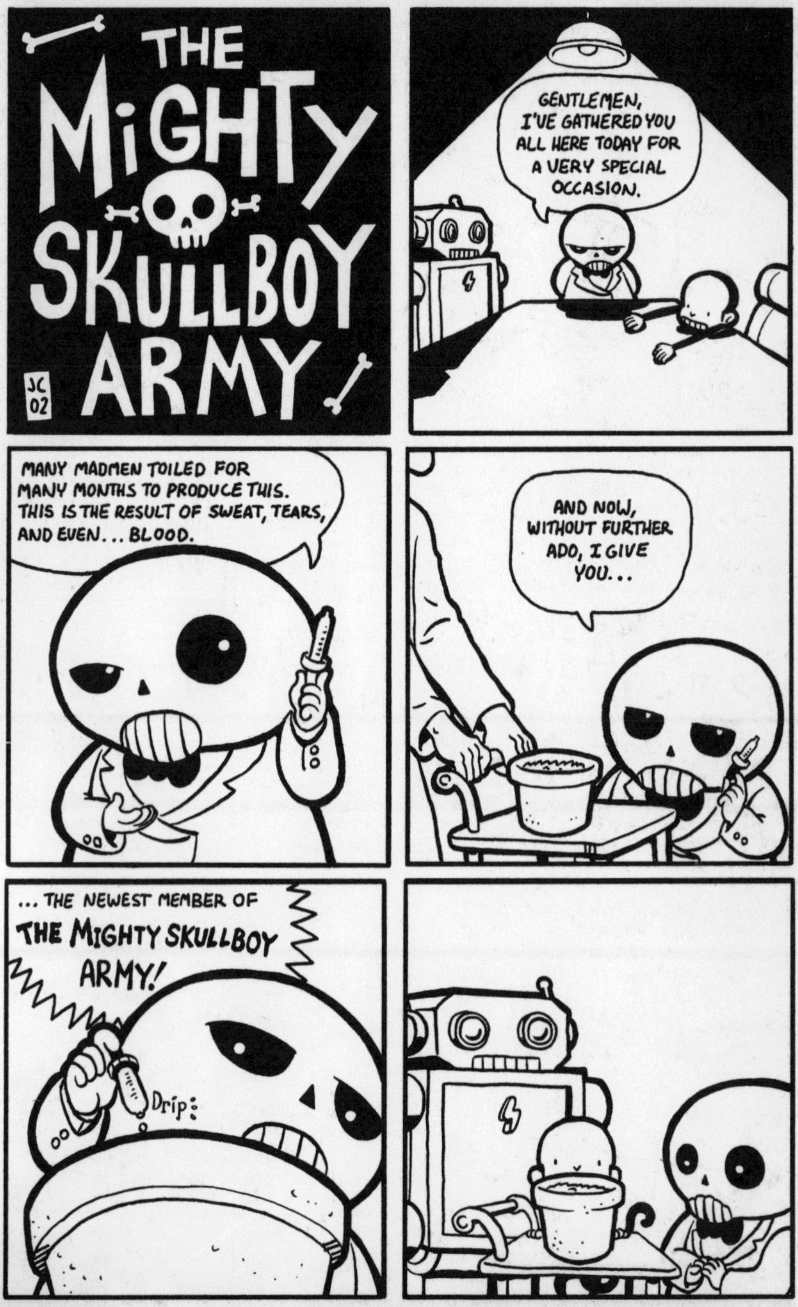
THE MIGHTY SKULLBOY ARMY
JC 02
GENTLEMEN, I'VE GATHERED YOU ALL HERE TODAY FOR A VERY SPECIAL OCCASION.
MANY MADMEN TOILED FOR MANY MONTHS TO PRODUCE THIS. THIS IS THE RESULT OF SWEAT, TEARS, AND EVEN... BLOOD.
AND NOW, WITHOUT FURTHER ADO, I GIVE YOU...
... THE NEWEST MEMBER OF THE MIGHTY SKULLBOY ARMY!
Drip

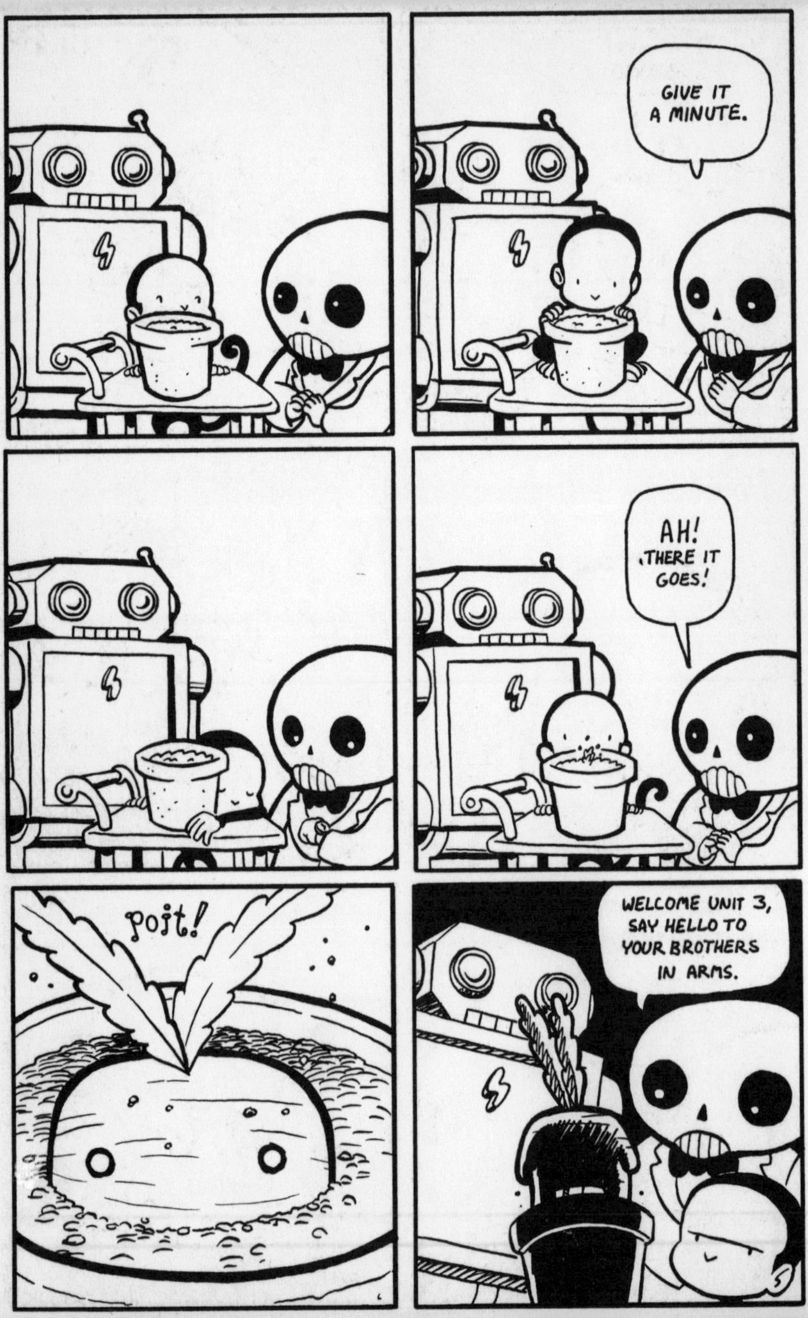
GIVE IT A MINUTE.
AH! THERE IT GOES!
poit!
WELCOME UNIT 3, SAY HELLO TO YOUR BROTHERS IN ARMS.

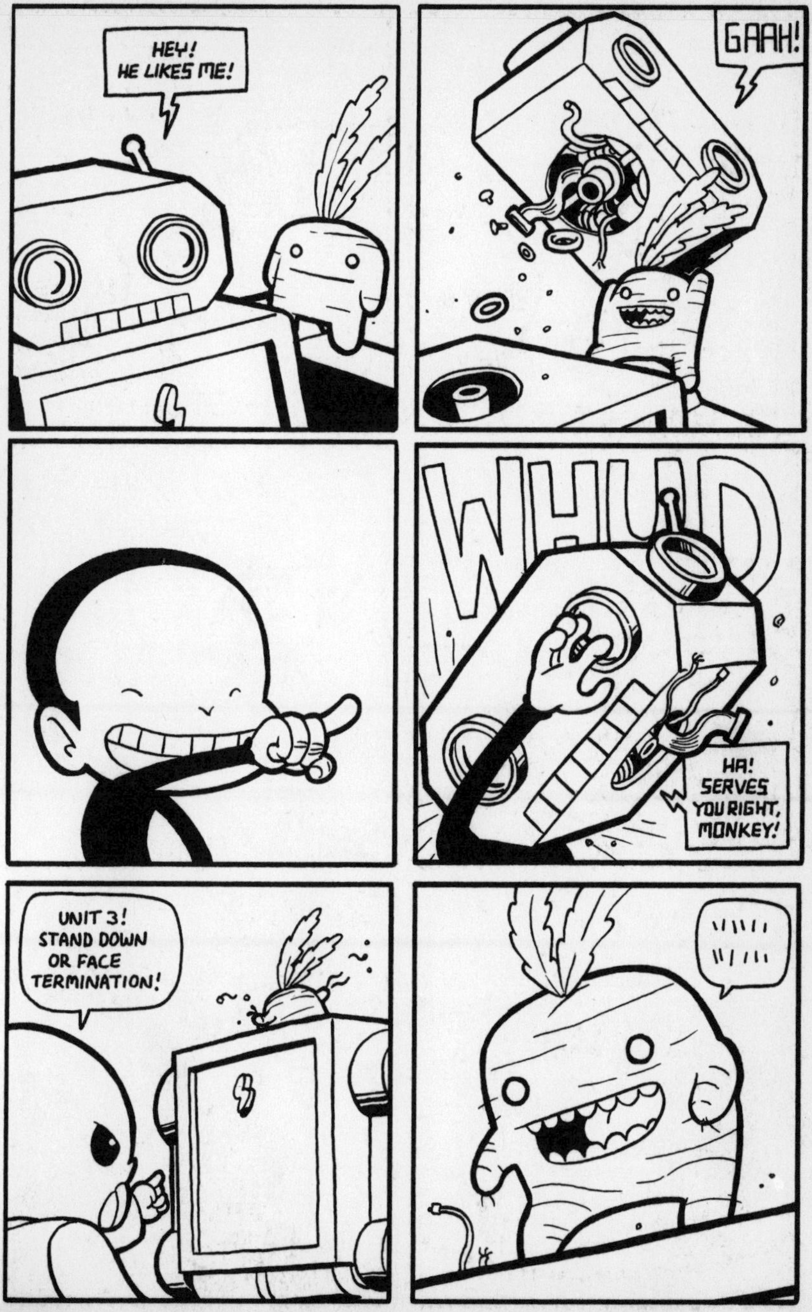
HEY! HE LIKES ME!
GAAH!
WHUD
HA! SERVES YOU RIGHT, MONKEY!
UNIT 3! STAND DOWN OR FACE TERMINATION!

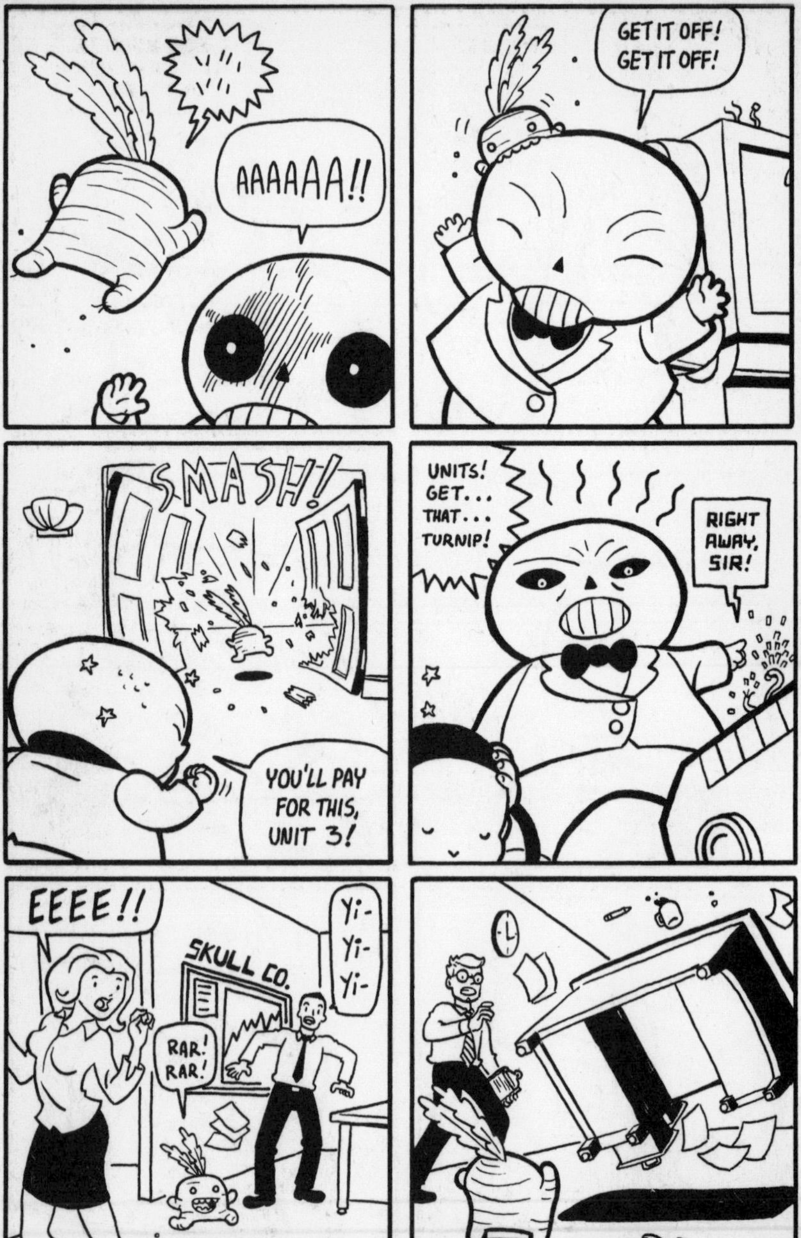
AAAAAA!!
GET IT OFF! GET IT OFF!
SMASH!
YOU'LL PAY FOR THIS, UNIT 3!
UNITS! GET... THAT... TURNIP!
RIGHT AWAY, SIR!
EEEE!!
SKULL CO.
RAR! RAR!
Yi- Yi- Yi-
FLiP!

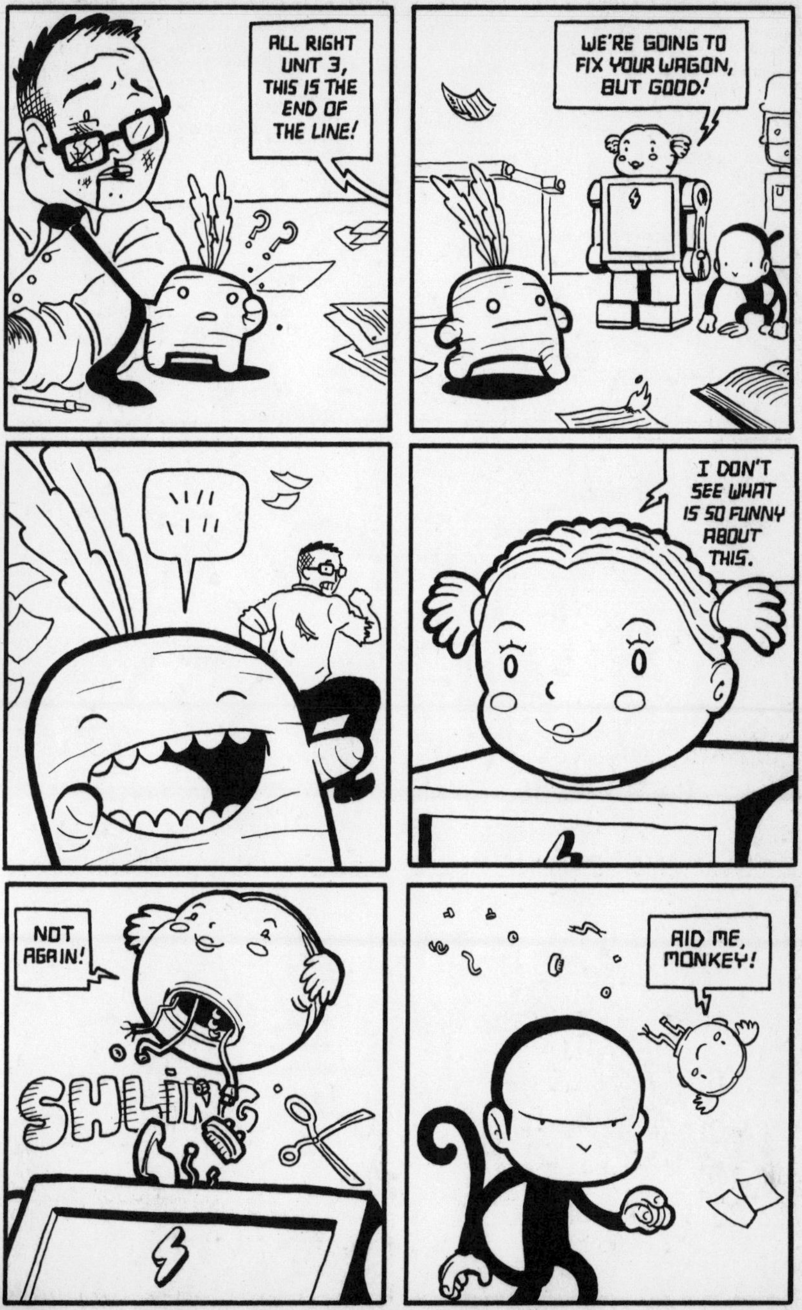
ALL RIGHT UNIT 3, THIS IS THE END OF THE LINE!
WE'RE GOING TO FIX YOUR WAGON, BUT GOOD!
I DON'T SEE WHAT IS SO FUNNY ABOUT THIS.
NOT AGAIN!
SHLING
AID ME, MONKEY!

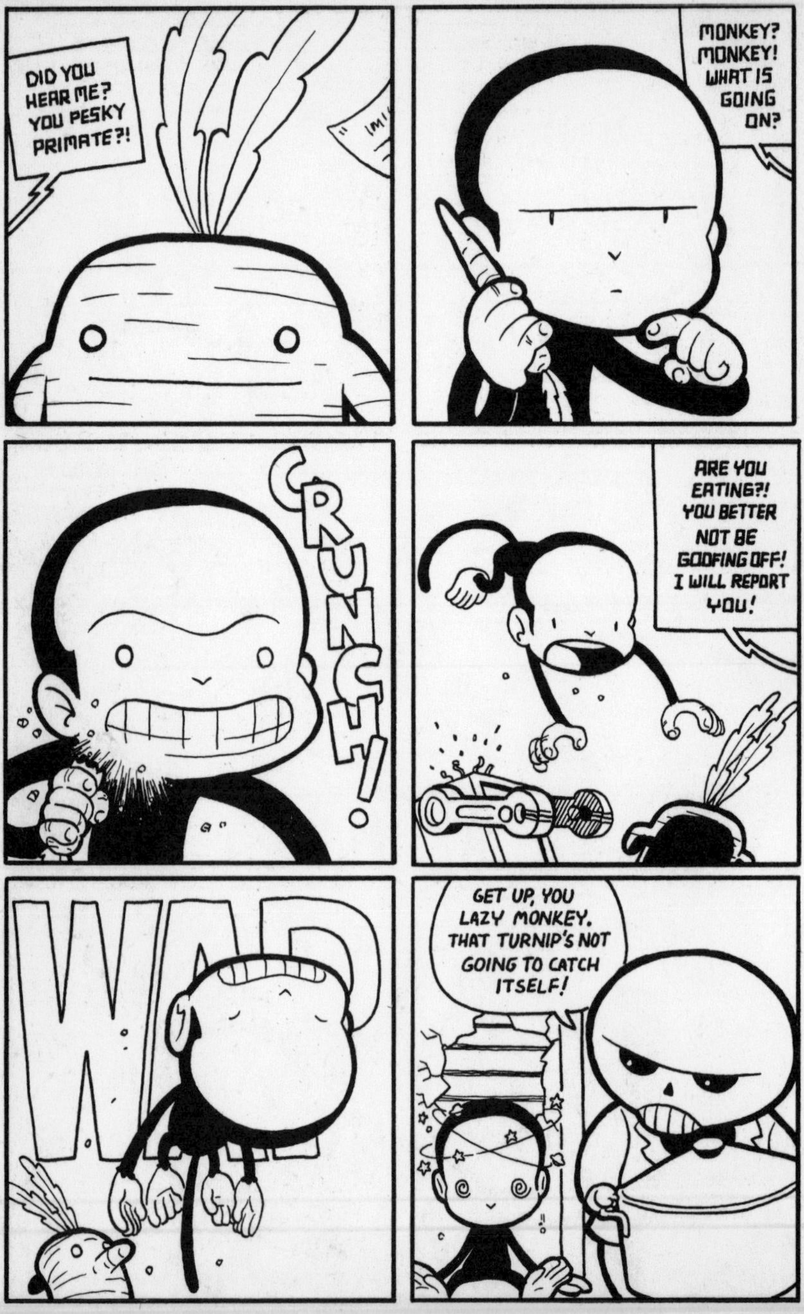
DID YOU HEAR ME? YOU PESKY PRIMATE?!
MONKEY? MONKEY! WHAT IS GOING ON?
CRUNCH!
ARE YOU EATING?! YOU BETTER NOT BE GOOFING OFF! I WILL REPORT YOU!
WAP
GET UP, YOU LAZY MONKEY. THAT TURNIP'S NOT GOING TO CATCH ITSELF!

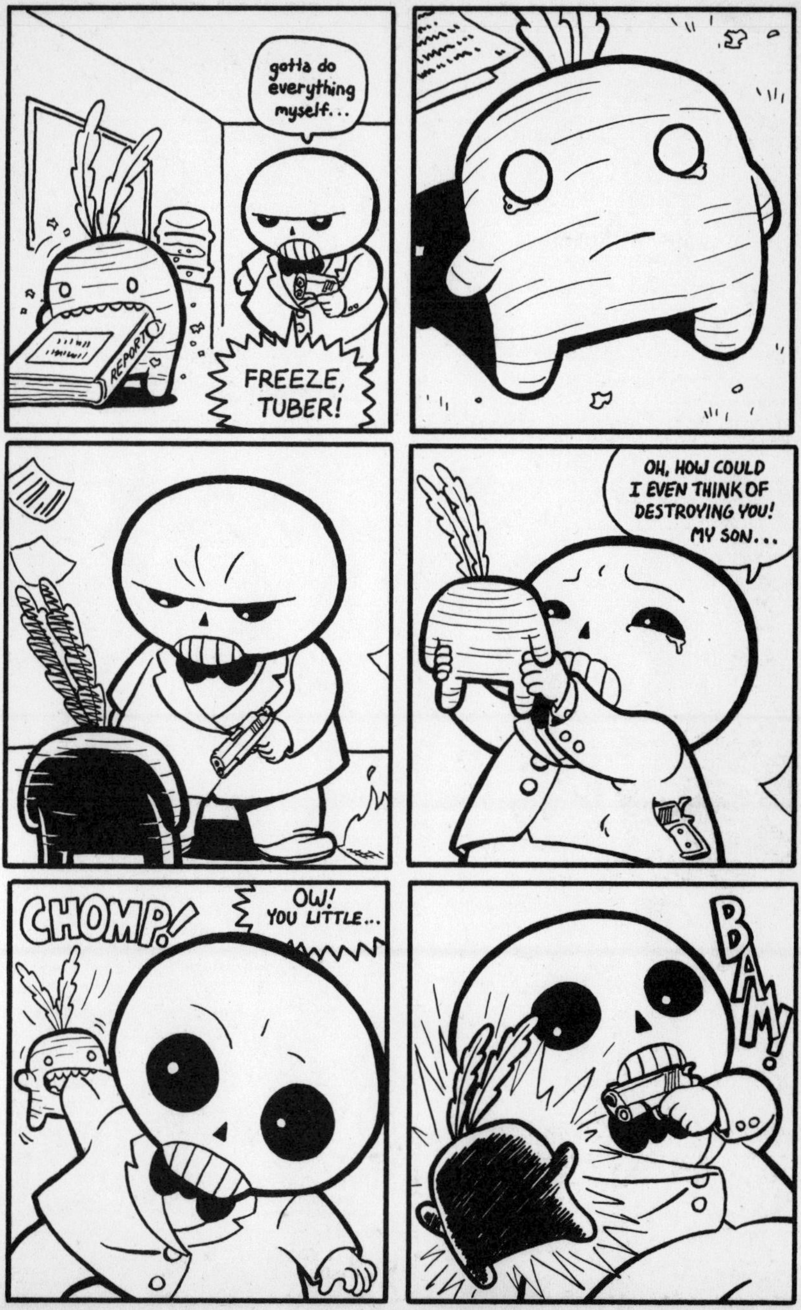
gotta do everything myself...
FREEZE, TUBER!
REPORT
OH, HOW COULD I EVEN THINK OF DESTROYING YOU! MY SON...
CHOMP!
OW! YOU LITTLE...
BAM!

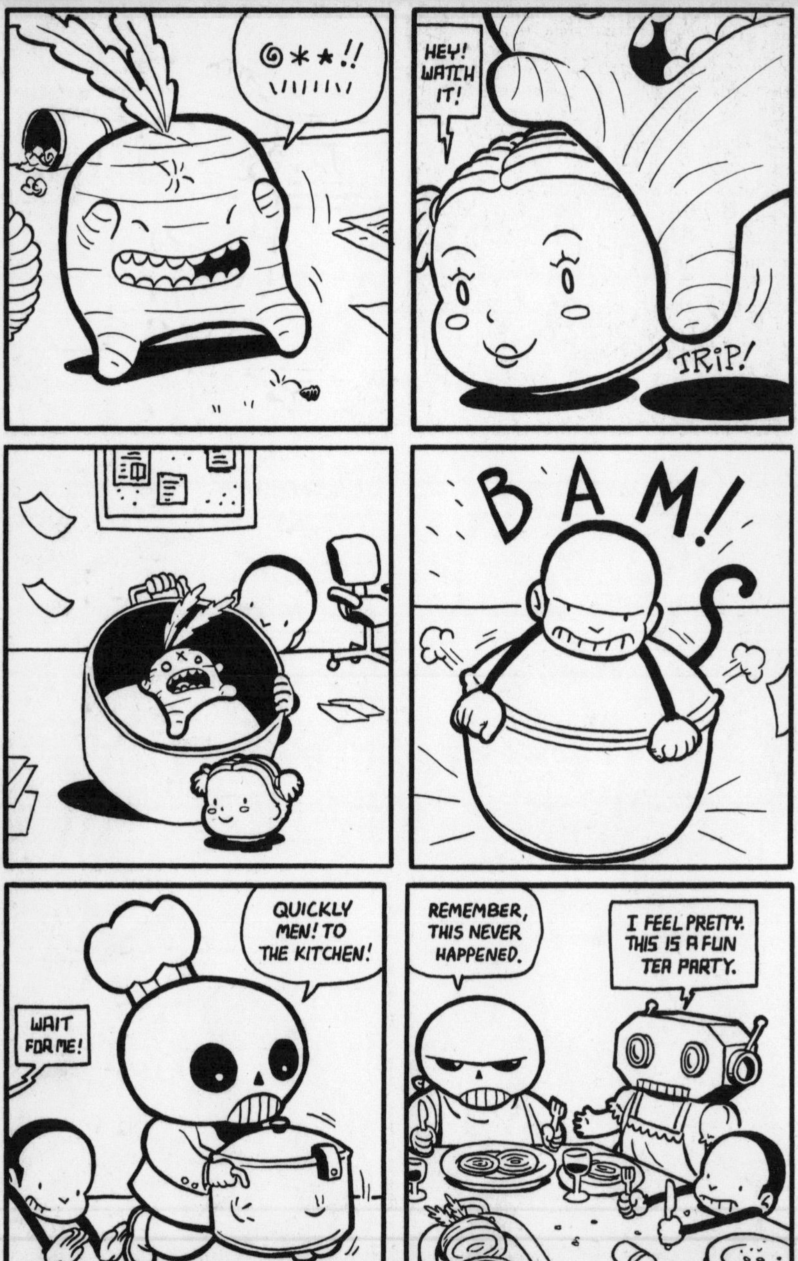
@*★!!
HEY! WATCH IT!
TRIP!
BAM!
QUICKLY MEN! TO THE KITCHEN!
WAIT FOR ME!
REMEMBER, THIS NEVER HAPPENED.
I FEEL PRETTY. THIS IS A FUN TEA PARTY.

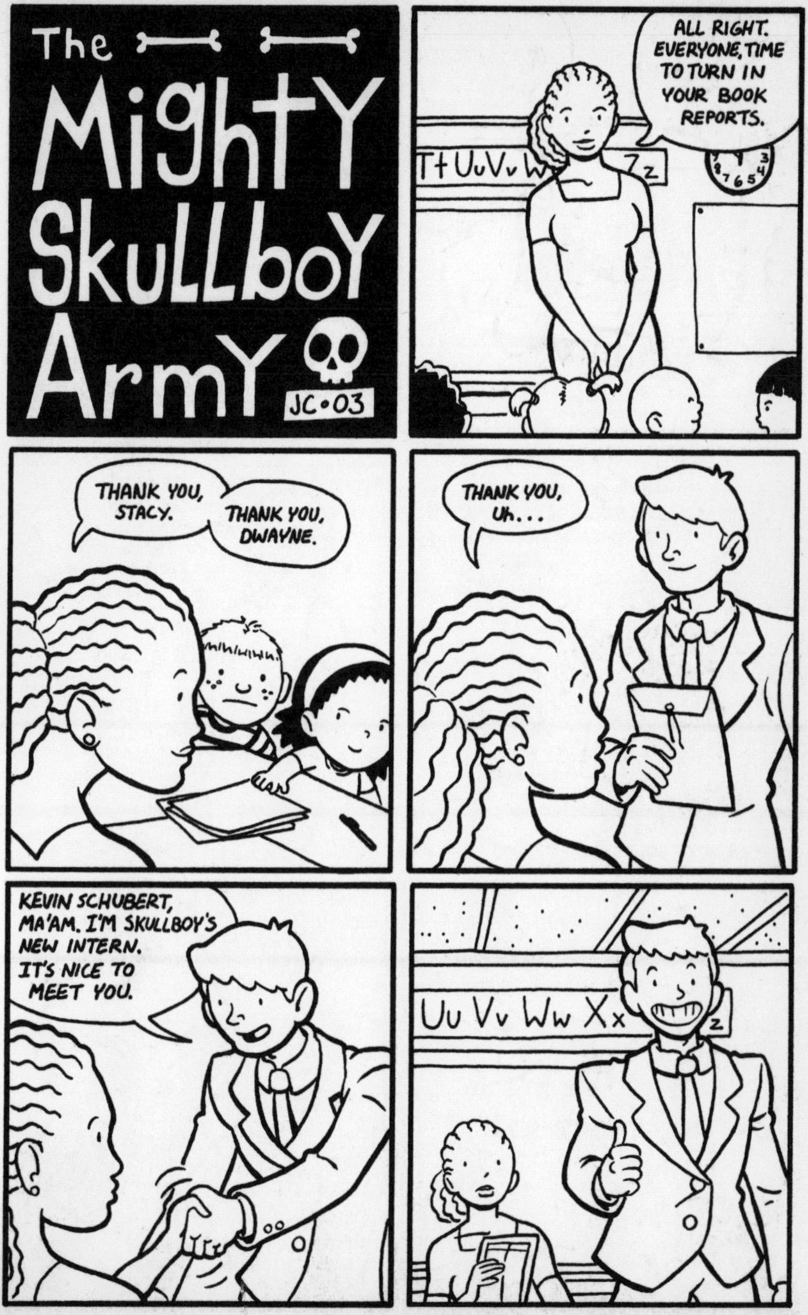
The
Mighty
Skullboy
Army
JC•03
ALL RIGHT. EVERYONE, TIME TO TURN IN YOUR BOOK REPORTS.
TtUuVvW
Zz
THANK YOU, STACY.
THANK YOU, DWAYNE.
THANK YOU, Uh...
KEVIN SCHUBERT, MA'AM. I'M SKULLBOY'S NEW INTERN. IT'S NICE TO MEET YOU.
Uu Vv Ww Xx
z

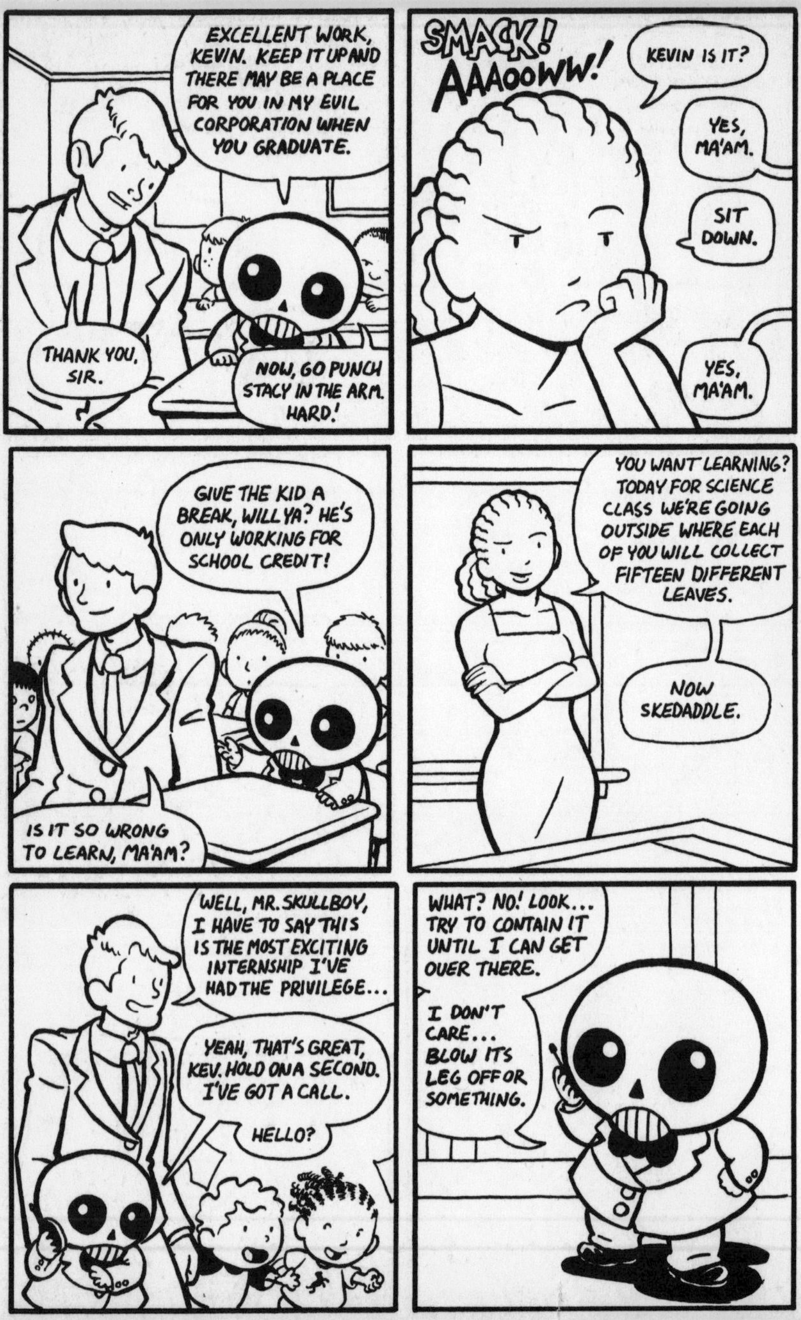

EXCELLENT WORK, KEVIN. KEEP IT UP AND THERE MAY BE A PLACE FOR YOU IN MY EVIL CORPORATION WHEN YOU GRADUATE.
THANK YOU, SIR.
NOW, GO PUNCH STACY IN THE ARM. HARD!
SMACK!
AAAOOWW!
KEVIN IS IT?
YES, MA'AM.
SIT DOWN.
YES, MA'AM.
GIVE THE KID A BREAK, WILL YA? HE'S ONLY WORKING FOR SCHOOL CREDIT!
IS IT SO WRONG TO LEARN, MA'AM?
YOU WANT LEARNING? TODAY FOR SCIENCE CLASS WE'RE GOING OUTSIDE WHERE EACH OF YOU WILL COLLECT FIFTEEN DIFFERENT LEAVES.
NOW SKEDADDLE.
WELL, MR. SKULLBOY, I HAVE TO SAY THIS IS THE MOST EXCITING INTERNSHIP I'VE HAD THE PRIVILEGE...
YEAH, THAT'S GREAT, KEV. HOLD ON A SECOND. I'VE GOT A CALL.
HELLO?
WHAT? NO! LOOK... TRY TO CONTAIN IT UNTIL I CAN GET OVER THERE.
I DON'T CARE... BLOW ITS LEG OFF OR SOMETHING.

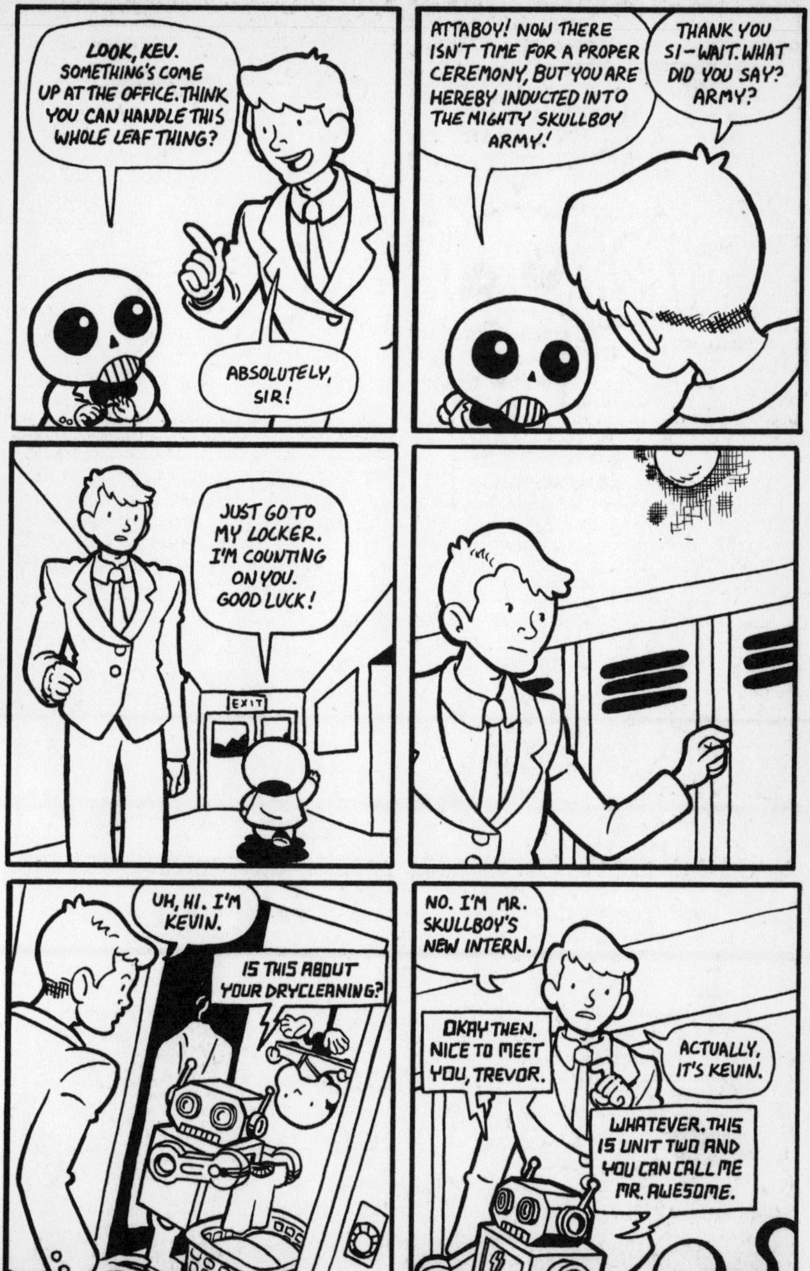
LOOK, KEV. SOMETHING'S COME UP AT THE OFFICE. THINK YOU CAN HANDLE THIS WHOLE LEAF THING?
ABSOLUTELY, SIR!
ATTABOY! NOW THERE ISN'T TIME FOR A PROPER CEREMONY, BUT YOU ARE HEREBY INDUCTED INTO THE MIGHTY SKULLBOY ARMY!
THANK YOU SI– WAIT. WHAT DID YOU SAY? ARMY?
JUST GO TO MY LOCKER. I'M COUNTING ON YOU. GOOD LUCK!
EXIT
UH, HI. I'M KEVIN.
IS THIS ABOUT YOUR DRYCLEANING?
NO. I'M MR. SKULLBOY'S NEW INTERN.
OKAY THEN. NICE TO MEET YOU, TREVOR.
ACTUALLY, IT'S KEVIN.
WHATEVER. THIS IS UNIT TWO AND YOU CAN CALL ME MR. AWESOME.

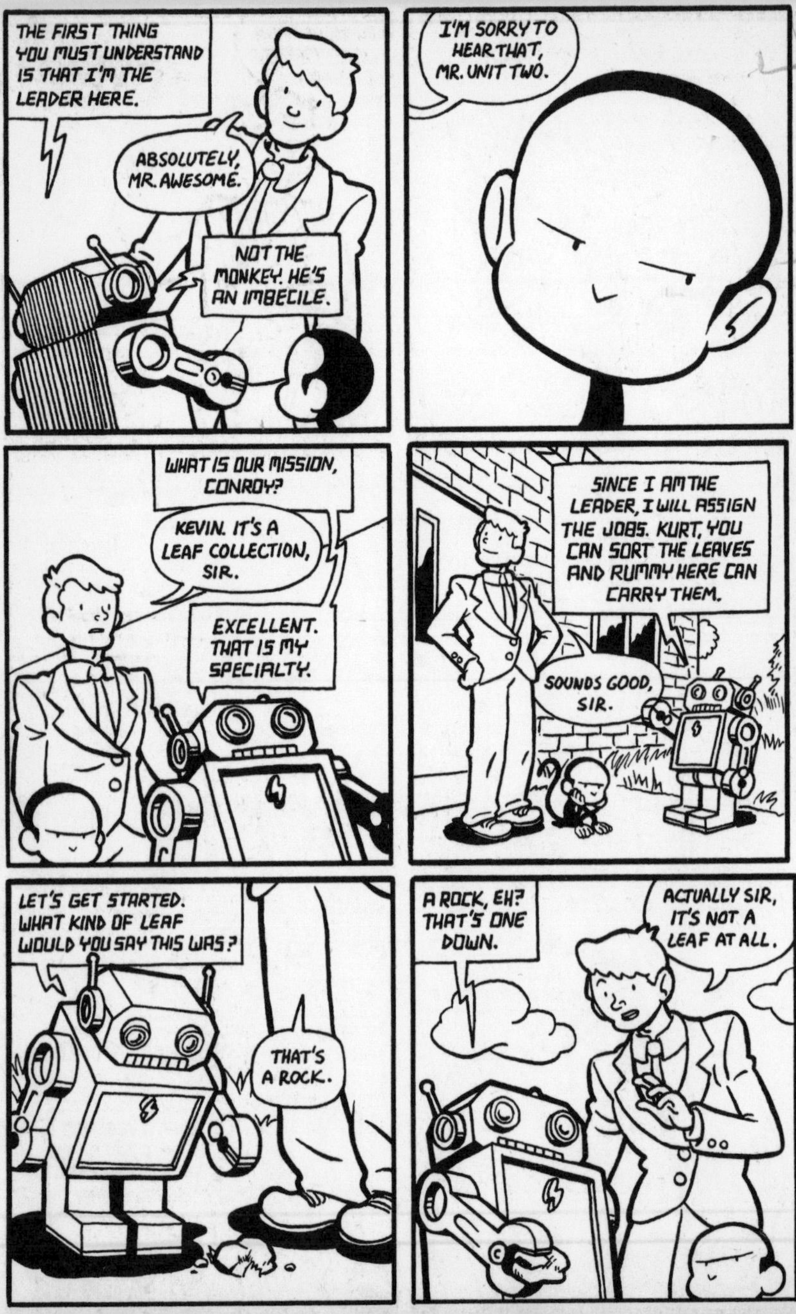
THE FIRST THING YOU MUST UNDERSTAND IS THAT I'M THE LEADER HERE.
ABSOLUTELY, MR. AWESOME.
NOT THE MONKEY. HE'S AN IMBECILE.
I'M SORRY TO HEAR THAT, MR. UNIT TWO.
WHAT IS OUR MISSION, CONROY?
KEVIN. IT'S A LEAF COLLECTION, SIR.
EXCELLENT. THAT IS MY SPECIALTY.
SINCE I AM THE LEADER, I WILL ASSIGN THE JOBS. KURT, YOU CAN SORT THE LEAVES AND RUMMY HERE CAN CARRY THEM.
SOUNDS GOOD, SIR.
LET'S GET STARTED. WHAT KIND OF LEAF WOULD YOU SAY THIS WAS?
THAT'S A ROCK.
A ROCK, EH? THAT'S ONE DOWN.
ACTUALLY SIR, IT'S NOT A LEAF AT ALL.

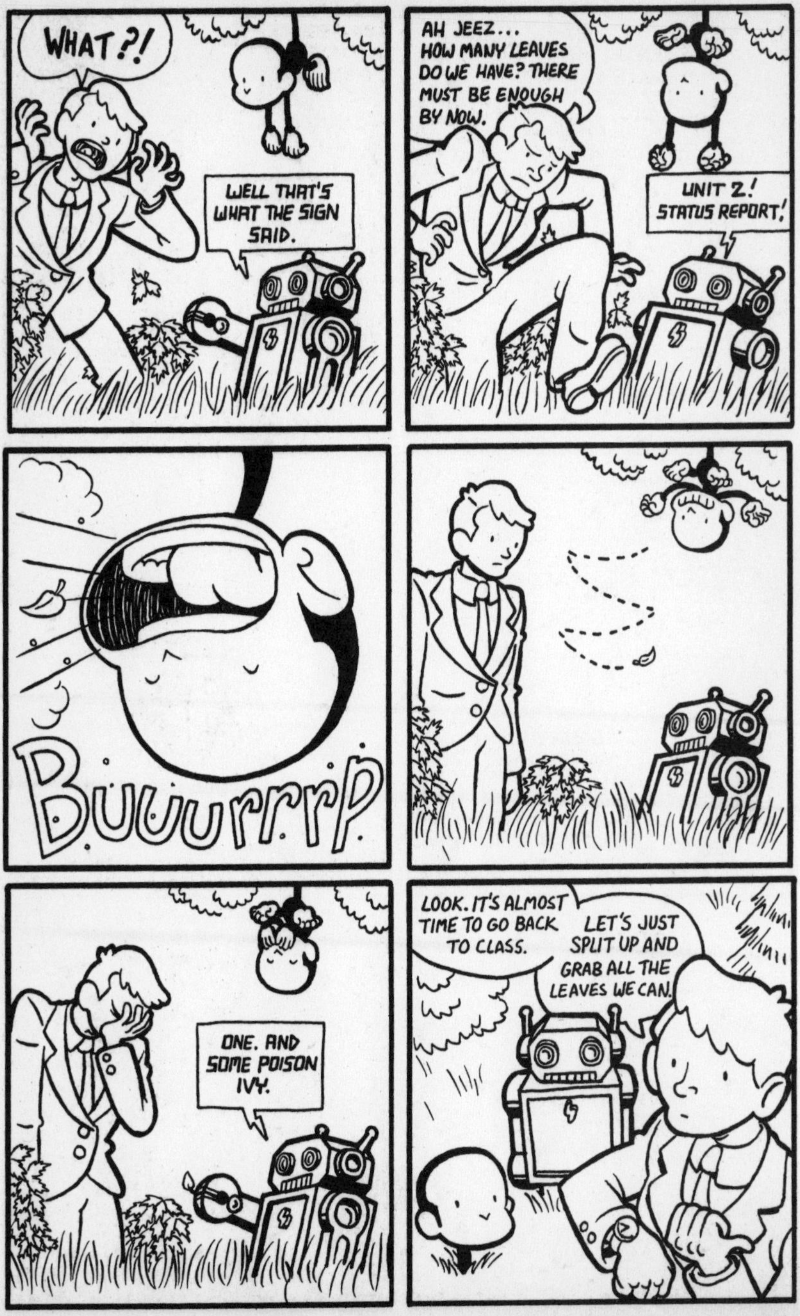
WHAT?!
WELL THAT'S WHAT THE SIGN SAID.
AH JEEZ... HOW MANY LEAVES DO WE HAVE? THERE MUST BE ENOUGH BY NOW.
UNIT 2! STATUS REPORT!
Buuurrrp
ONE. AND SOME POISON IVY.
LOOK. IT'S ALMOST TIME TO GO BACK TO CLASS.
LET'S JUST SPLIT UP AND GRAB ALL THE LEAVES WE CAN.

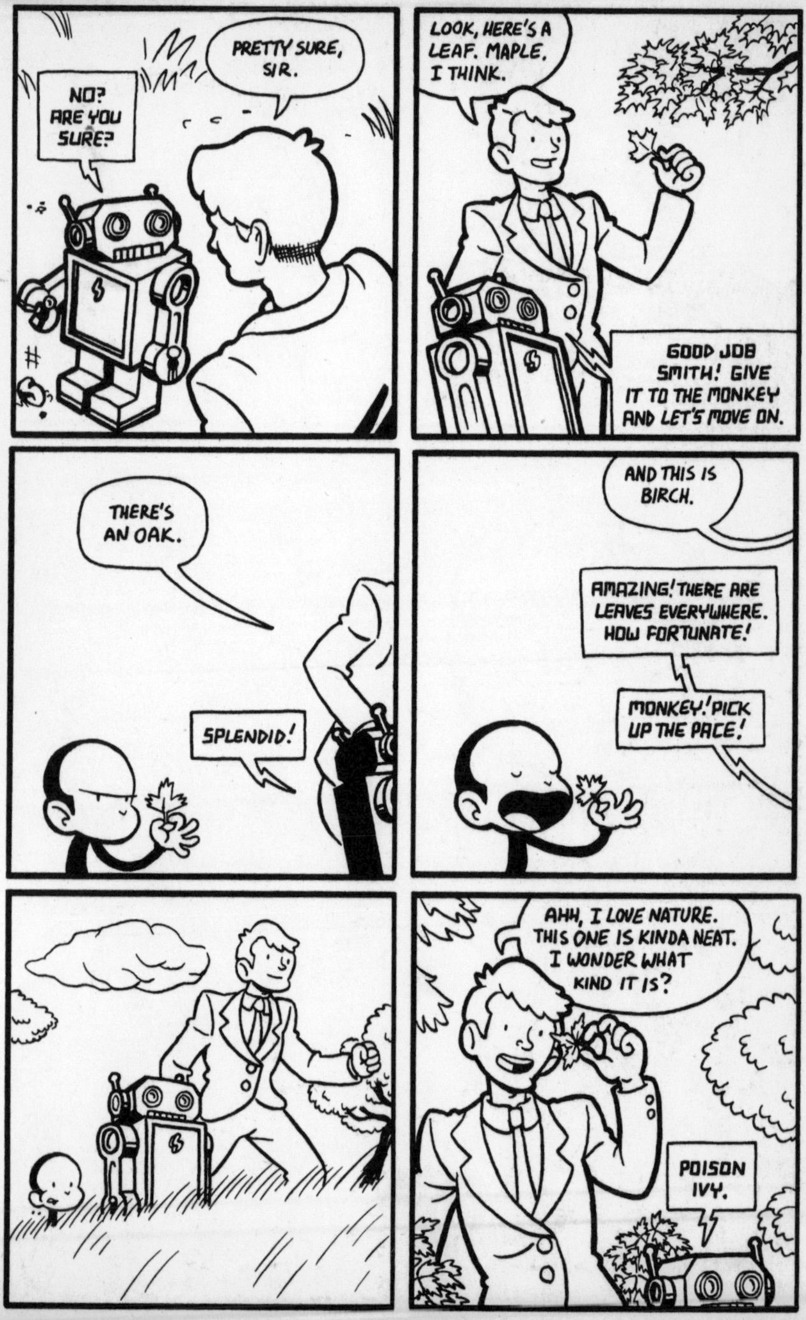

NO? ARE YOU SURE?
PRETTY SURE, SIR.
LOOK, HERE'S A LEAF. MAPLE. I THINK.
GOOD JOB SMITH! GIVE IT TO THE MONKEY AND LET'S MOVE ON.
THERE'S AN OAK.
SPLENDID!
AND THIS IS BIRCH.
AMAZING! THERE ARE LEAVES EVERYWHERE. HOW FORTUNATE!
MONKEY! PICK UP THE PACE!
AHH, I LOVE NATURE. THIS ONE IS KINDA NEAT. I WONDER WHAT KIND IT IS?
POISON IVY.

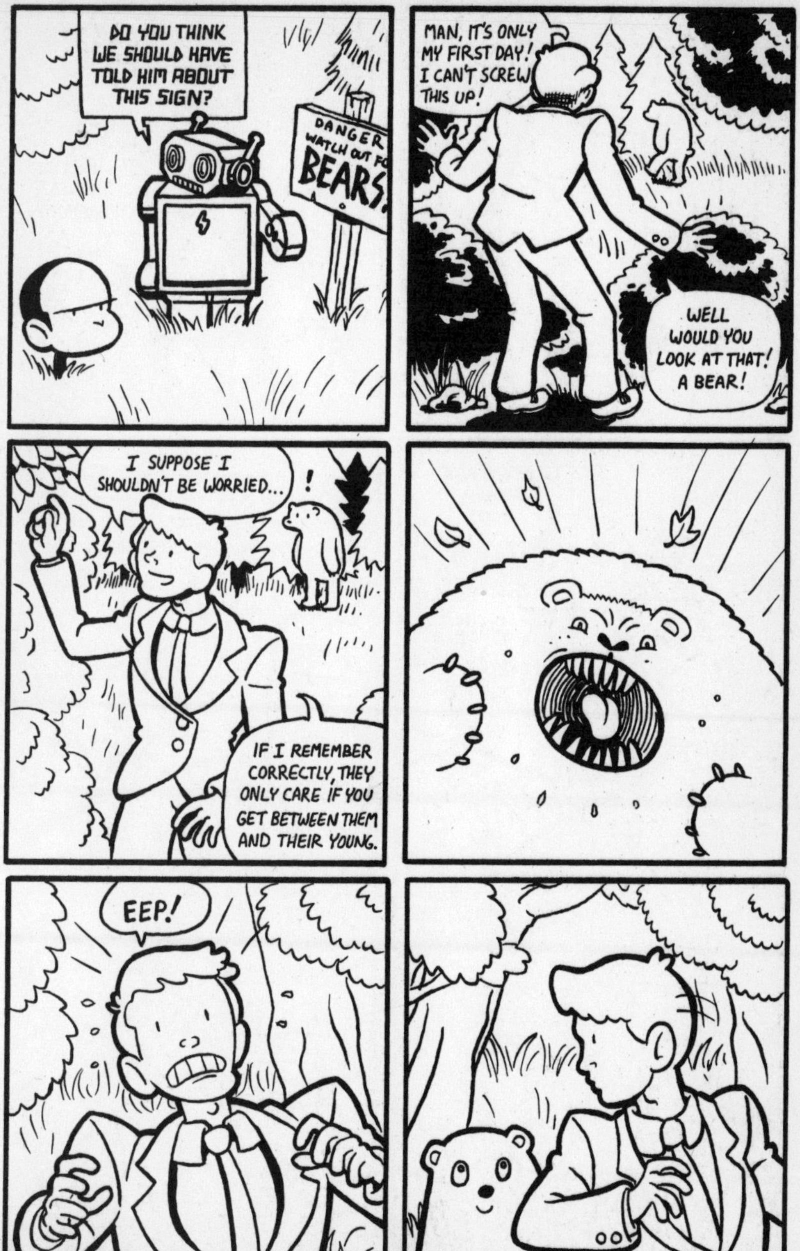
DO YOU THINK WE SHOULD HAVE TOLD HIM ABOUT THIS SIGN?
DANGER WATCH OUT FO BEARS
MAN, IT'S ONLY MY FIRST DAY! I CAN'T SCREW THIS UP!
WELL WOULD YOU LOOK AT THAT! A BEAR!
I SUPPOSE I SHOULDN'T BE WORRIED...
!
IF I REMEMBER CORRECTLY, THEY ONLY CARE IF YOU GET BETWEEN THEM AND THEIR YOUNG.
EEP!

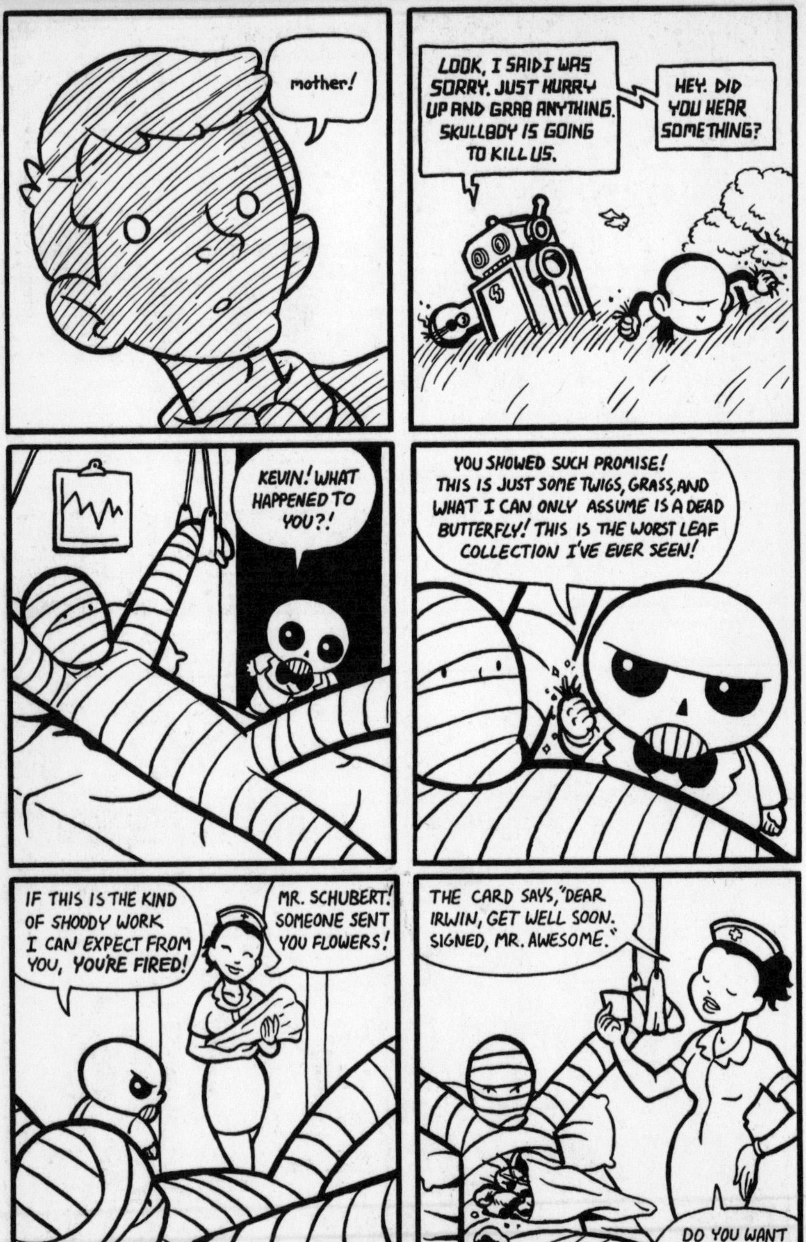
mother!
LOOK, I SAID I WAS SORRY. JUST HURRY UP AND GRAB ANYTHING. SKULLBOY IS GOING TO KILL US.
HEY. DID YOU HEAR SOMETHING?
KEVIN! WHAT HAPPENED TO YOU?!
YOU SHOWED SUCH PROMISE! THIS IS JUST SOME TWIGS, GRASS, AND WHAT I CAN ONLY ASSUME IS A DEAD BUTTERFLY! THIS IS THE WORST LEAF COLLECTION I'VE EVER SEEN!
IF THIS IS THE KIND OF SHODDY WORK I CAN EXPECT FROM YOU, YOU'RE FIRED!
MR. SCHUBERT! SOMEONE SENT YOU FLOWERS!
THE CARD SAYS, "DEAR IRWIN, GET WELL SOON. SIGNED, MR. AWESOME."
DO YOU WANT ME TO PUT THOSE IN WATER?

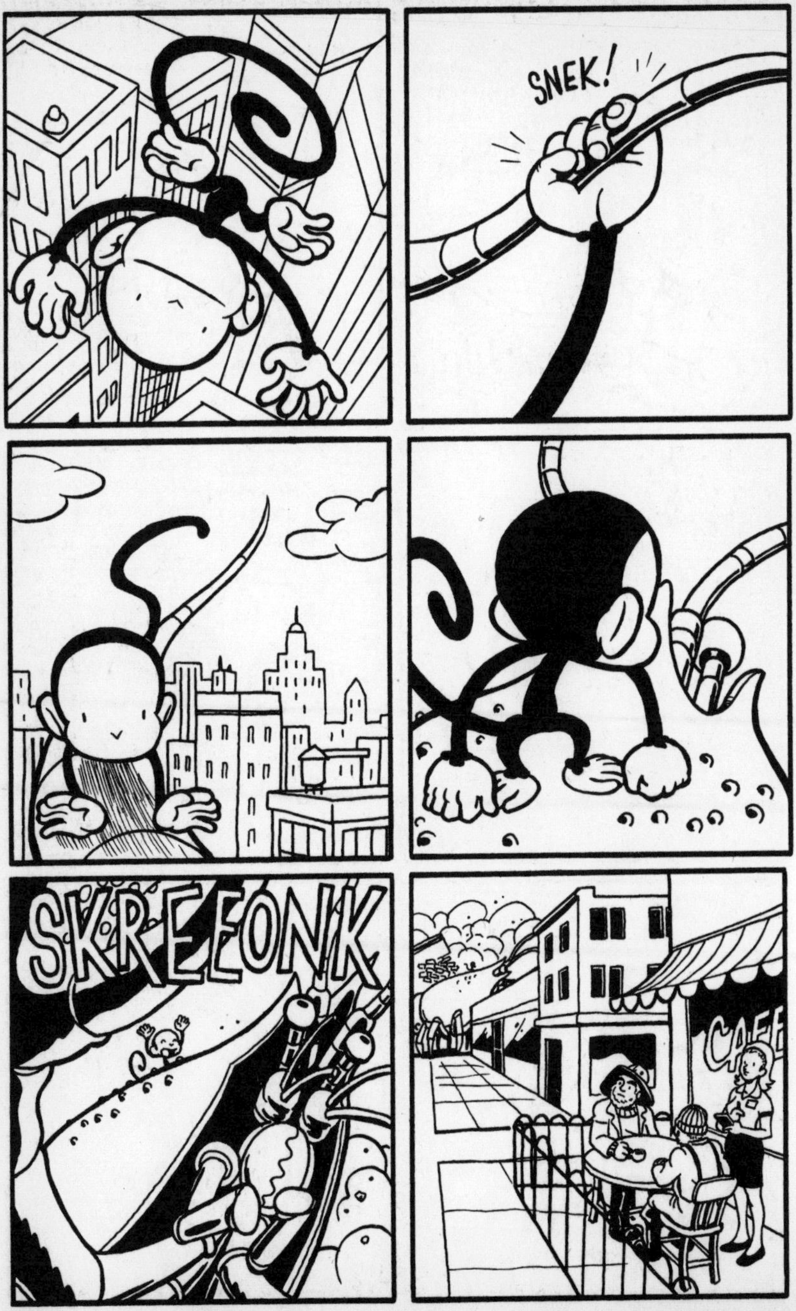
SNEK!
SKREEONK
CAFE

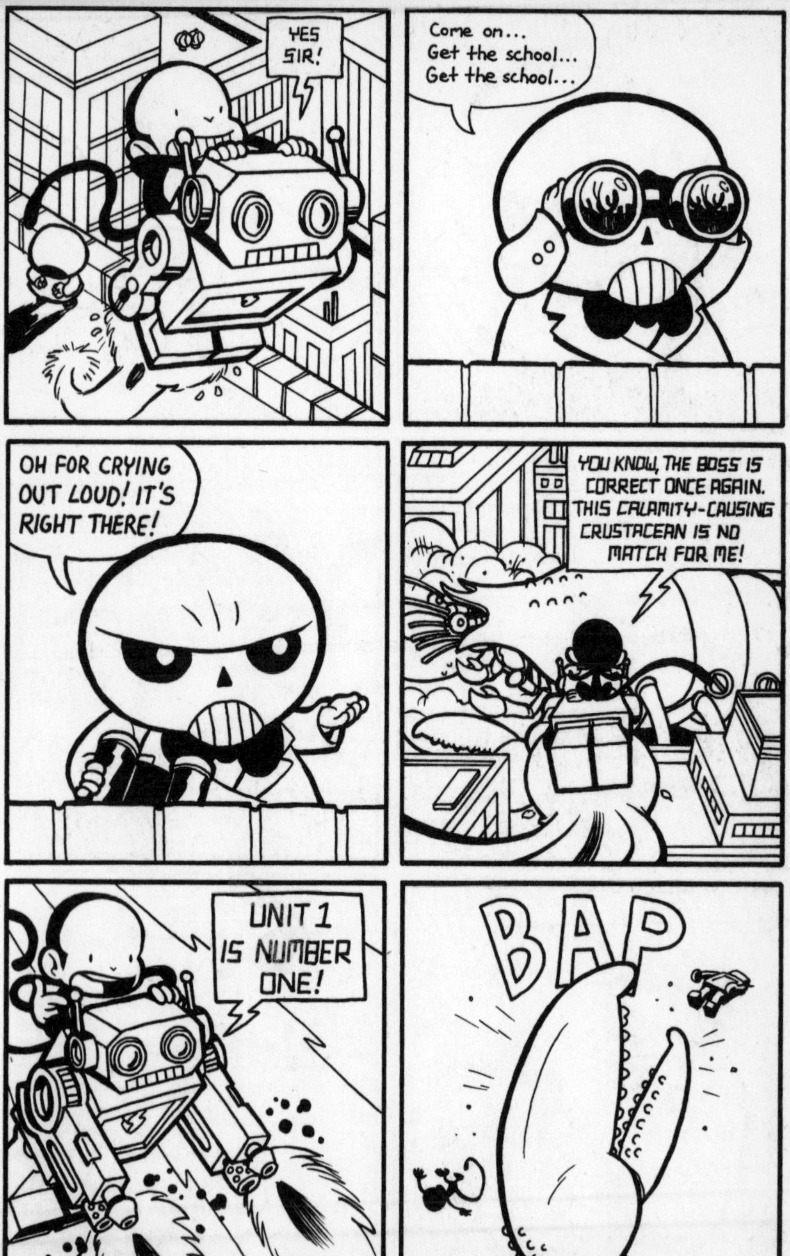
YES SIR!
Come on... Get the school... Get the school...
OH FOR CRYING OUT LOUD! IT'S RIGHT THERE!
YOU KNOW, THE BOSS IS CORRECT ONCE AGAIN. THIS CALAMITY-CAUSING CRUSTACEAN IS NO MATCH FOR ME!
UNIT 1 IS NUMBER ONE!
BAP

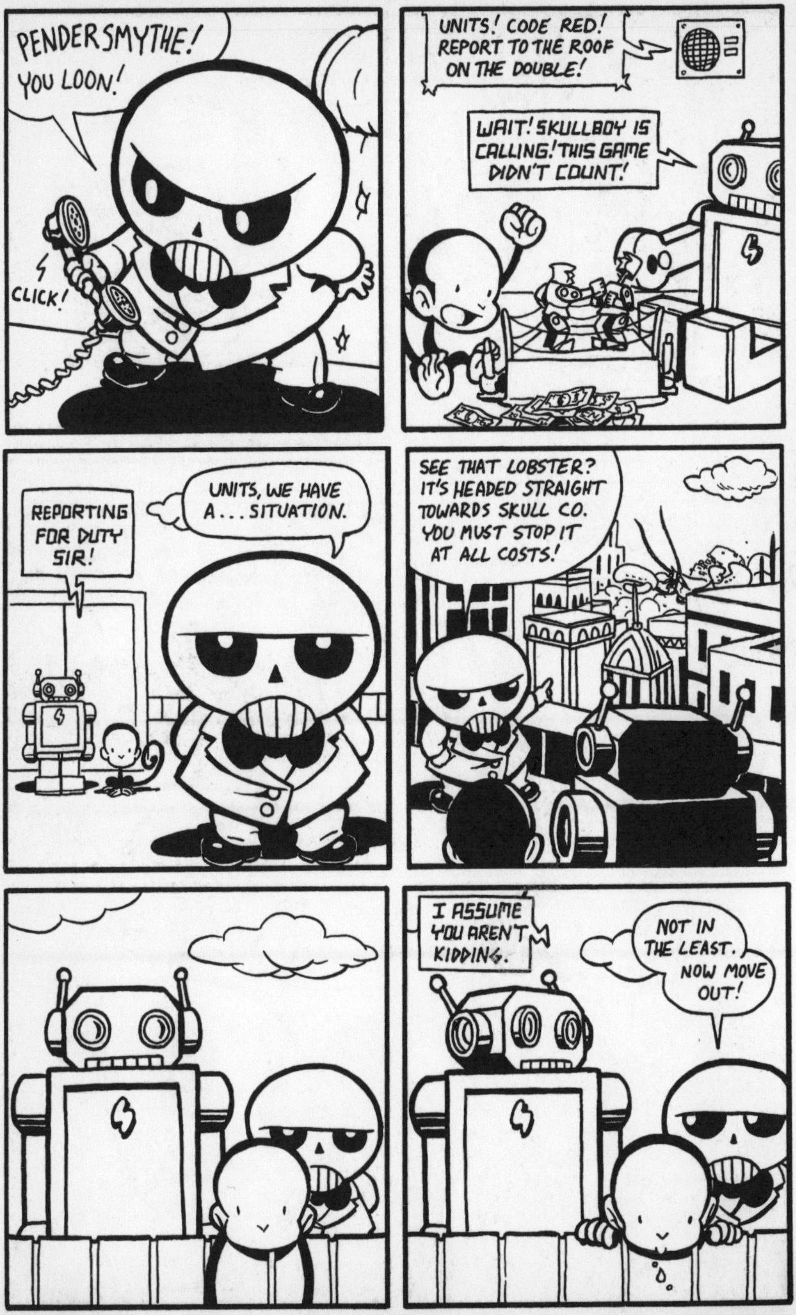
PENDERSMYTHE! YOU LOON!
CLICK!
UNITS! CODE RED! REPORT TO THE ROOF ON THE DOUBLE!
WAIT! SKULLBOY IS CALLING! THIS GAME DIDN'T COUNT!
REPORTING FOR DUTY SIR!
UNITS, WE HAVE A . . . SITUATION.
SEE THAT LOBSTER? IT'S HEADED STRAIGHT TOWARDS SKULL CO. YOU MUST STOP IT AT ALL COSTS!
I ASSUME YOU AREN'T KIDDING.
NOT IN THE LEAST. NOW MOVE OUT!

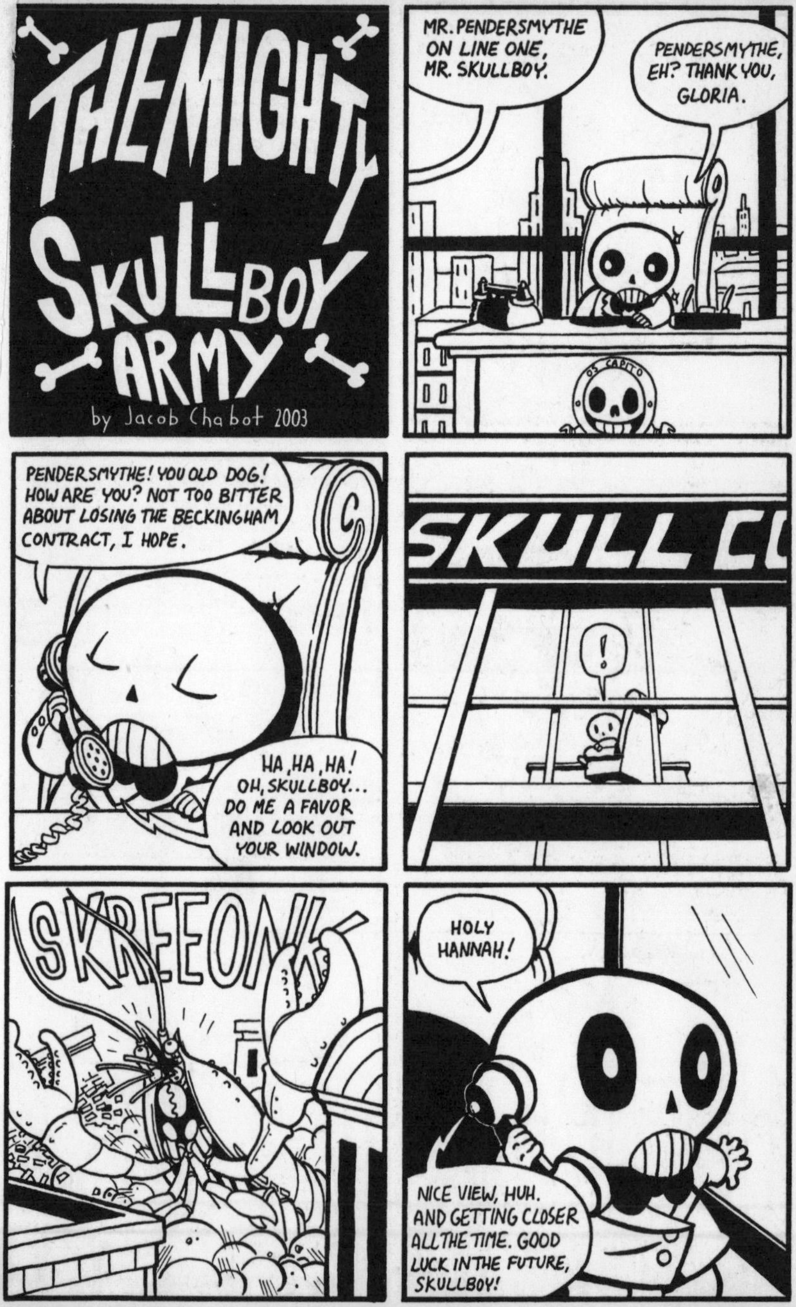
THE MIGHTY SKULLBOY ARMY
by Jacob Chabot 2003
MR. PENDERSMYTHE ON LINE ONE, MR. SKULLBOY.
PENDERSMYTHE, EH? THANK YOU, GLORIA.
PENDERSMYTHE! YOU OLD DOG! HOW ARE YOU? NOT TOO BITTER ABOUT LOSING THE BECKINGHAM CONTRACT, I HOPE.
HA, HA, HA! OH, SKULLBOY... DO ME A FAVOR AND LOOK OUT YOUR WINDOW.
SKULL CO
!
SKREEONK
HOLY HANNAH!
NICE VIEW, HUH. AND GETTING CLOSER ALL THE TIME. GOOD LUCK IN THE FUTURE, SKULLBOY!

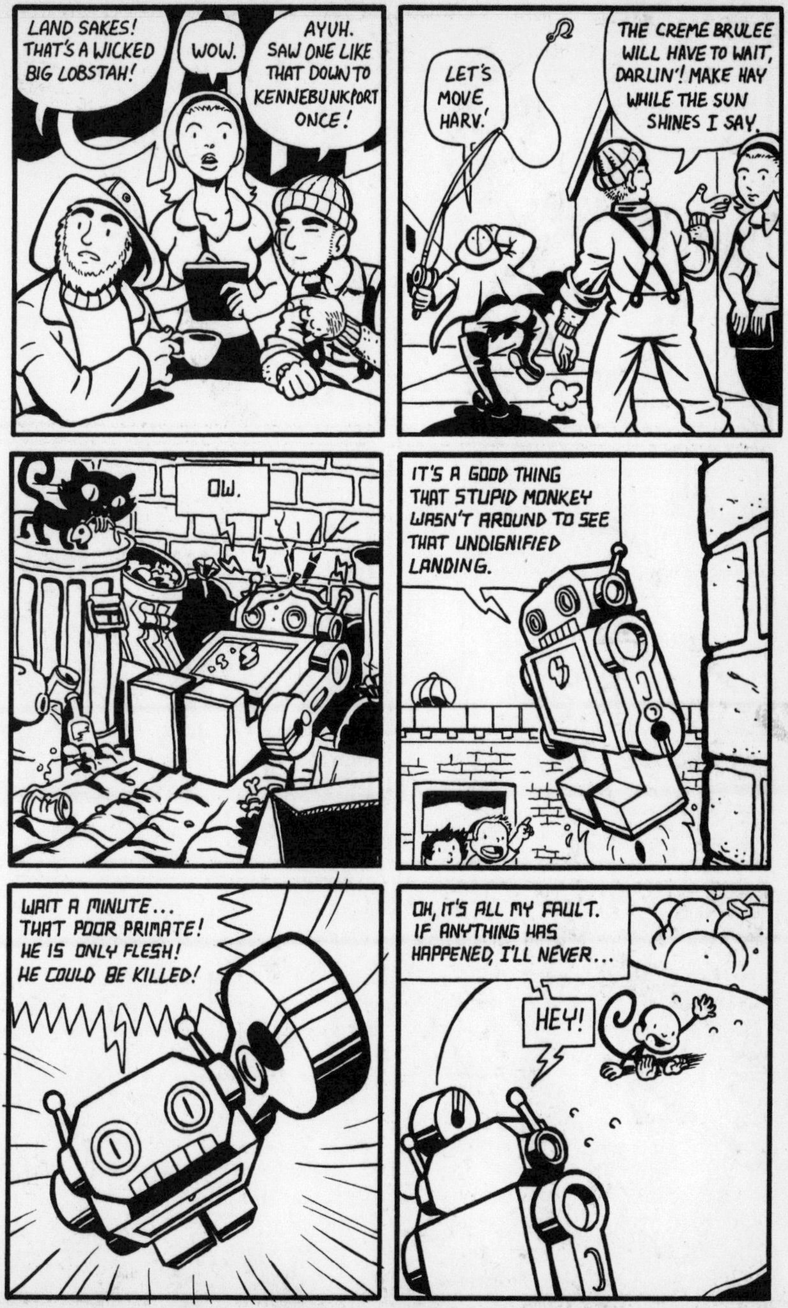
LAND SAKES! THAT'S A WICKED BIG LOBSTAH!
WOW.
AYUH. SAW ONE LIKE THAT DOWN TO KENNEBUNKPORT ONCE!
LET'S MOVE HARV.!
THE CREME BRULEE WILL HAVE TO WAIT, DARLIN'! MAKE HAY WHILE THE SUN SHINES I SAY.
OW.
IT'S A GOOD THING THAT STUPID MONKEY WASN'T AROUND TO SEE THAT UNDIGNIFIED LANDING.
WAIT A MINUTE... THAT POOR PRIMATE! HE IS ONLY FLESH! HE COULD BE KILLED!
OH, IT'S ALL MY FAULT. IF ANYTHING HAS HAPPENED, I'LL NEVER...
HEY!

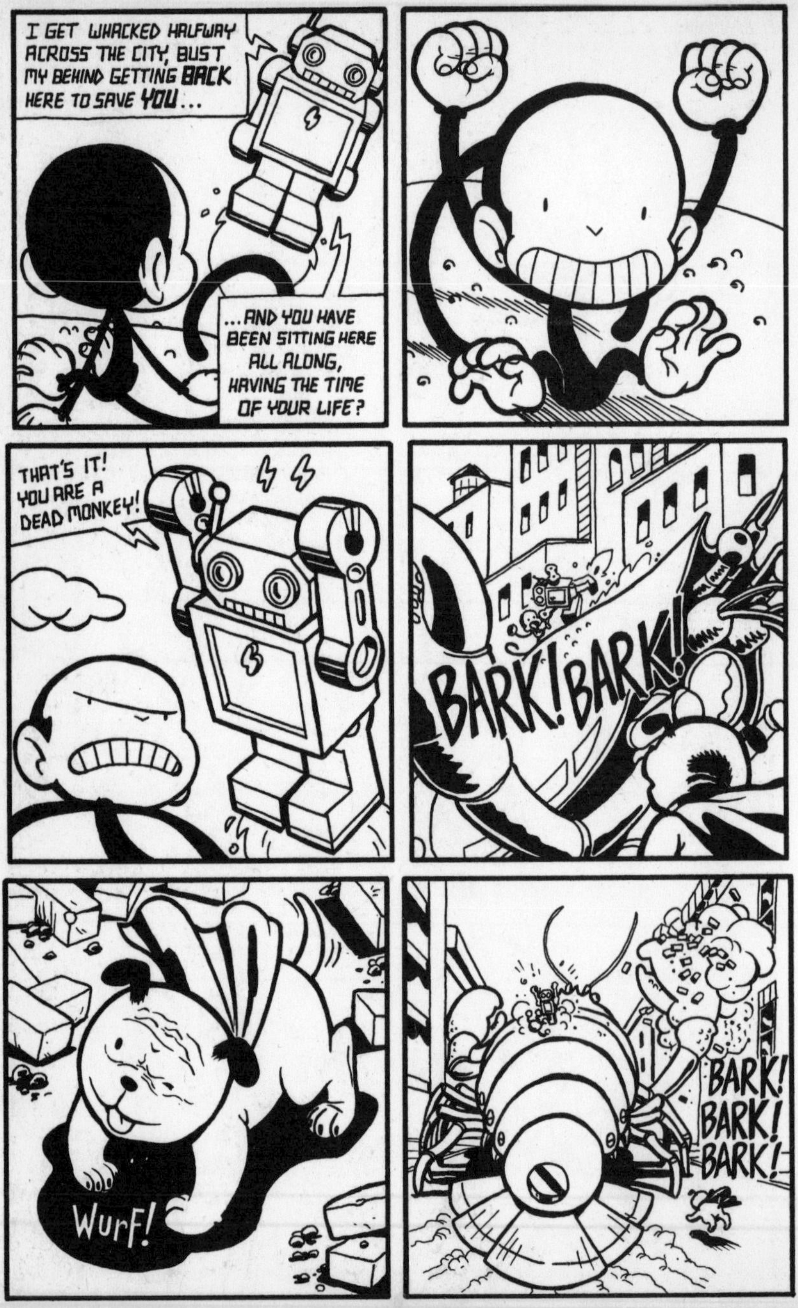
I GET WHACKED HALFWAY ACROSS THE CITY, BUST MY BEHIND GETTING BACK HERE TO SAVE YOU...
...AND YOU HAVE BEEN SITTING HERE ALL ALONG, HAVING THE TIME OF YOUR LIFE?
THAT'S IT! YOU ARE A DEAD MONKEY!
BARK! BARK!
WURF!
BARK!
BARK!
BARK!

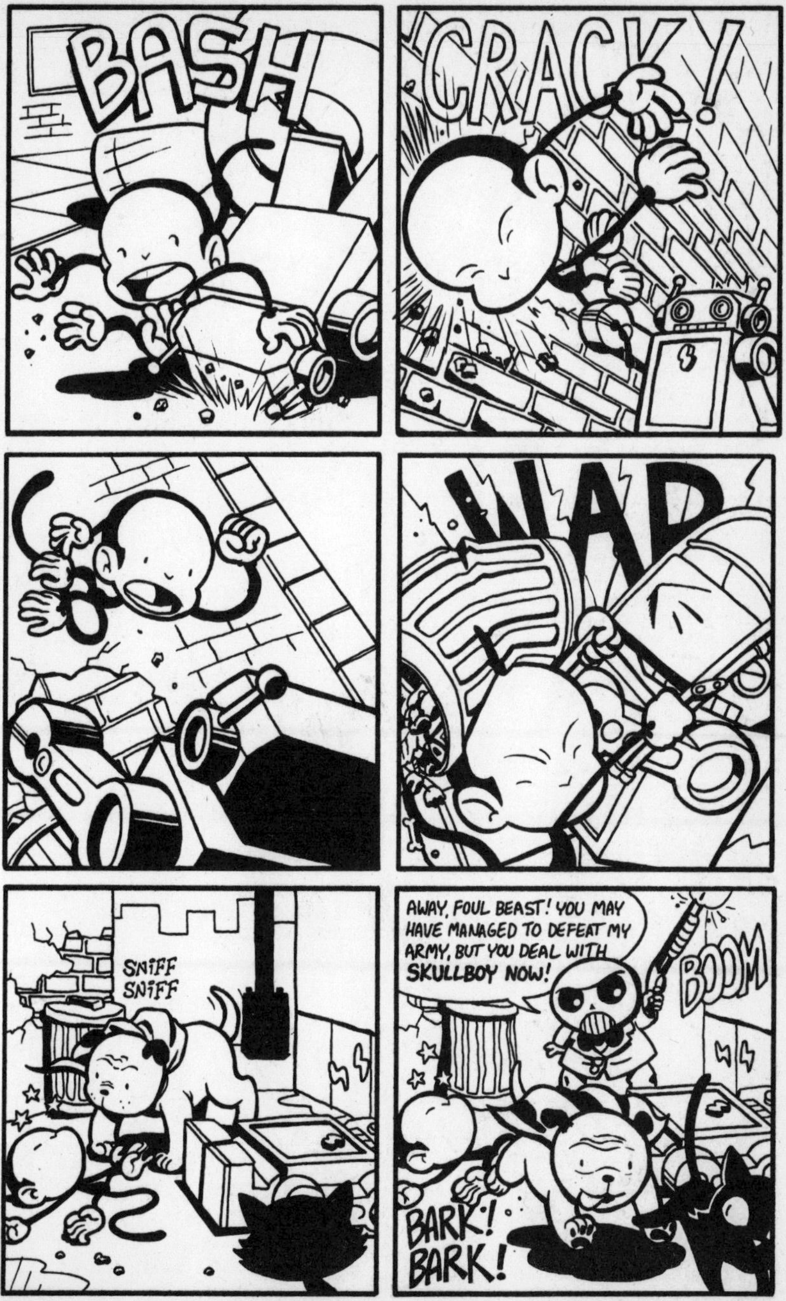
BASH
CRACK!
WAP
SNIFF SNIFF
AWAY, FOUL BEAST! YOU MAY HAVE MANAGED TO DEFEAT MY ARMY, BUT YOU DEAL WITH SKULLBOY NOW!
BOOM
BARK! BARK!

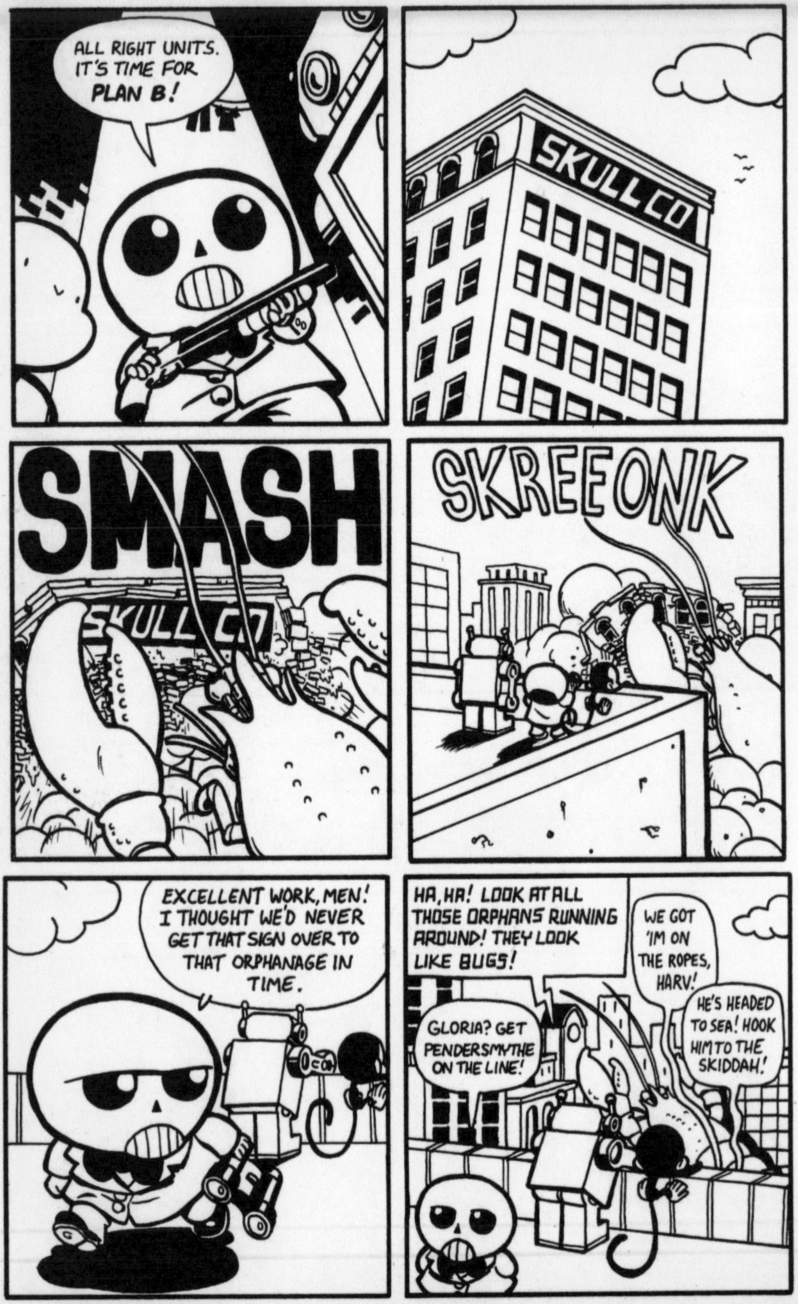
ALL RIGHT UNITS. IT'S TIME FOR PLAN B!
SKULLCO
SMASH
SKULL CO
SKREEONK
EXCELLENT WORK, MEN! I THOUGHT WE'D NEVER GET THAT SIGN OVER TO THAT ORPHANAGE IN TIME.
HA, HA! LOOK AT ALL THOSE ORPHANS RUNNING AROUND! THEY LOOK LIKE BUGS!
GLORIA? GET PENDERSMYTHE ON THE LINE!
WE GOT 'IM ON THE ROPES, HARV!
HE'S HEADED TO SEA! HOOK HIM TO THE SKIDDAH!

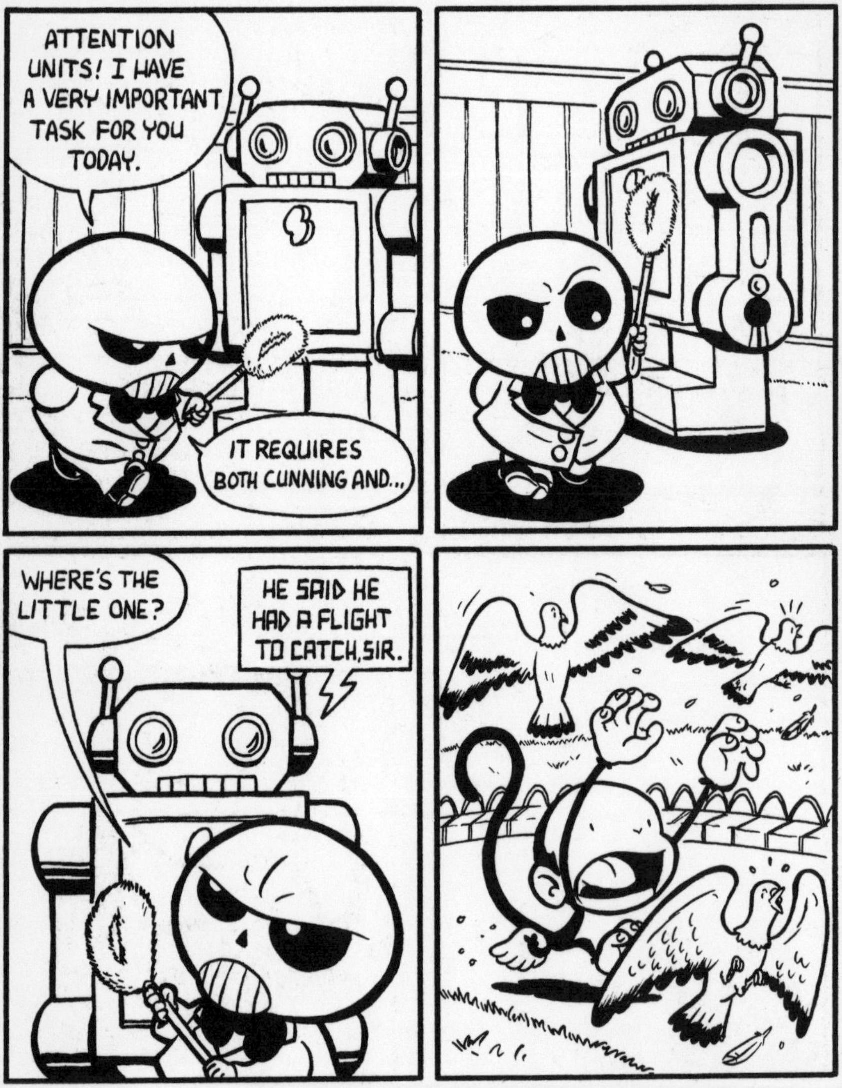
ATTENTION UNITS! I HAVE A VERY IMPORTANT TASK FOR YOU TODAY.
IT REQUIRES BOTH CUNNING AND...
WHERE'S THE LITTLE ONE?
HE SAID HE HAD A FLIGHT TO CATCH, SIR.

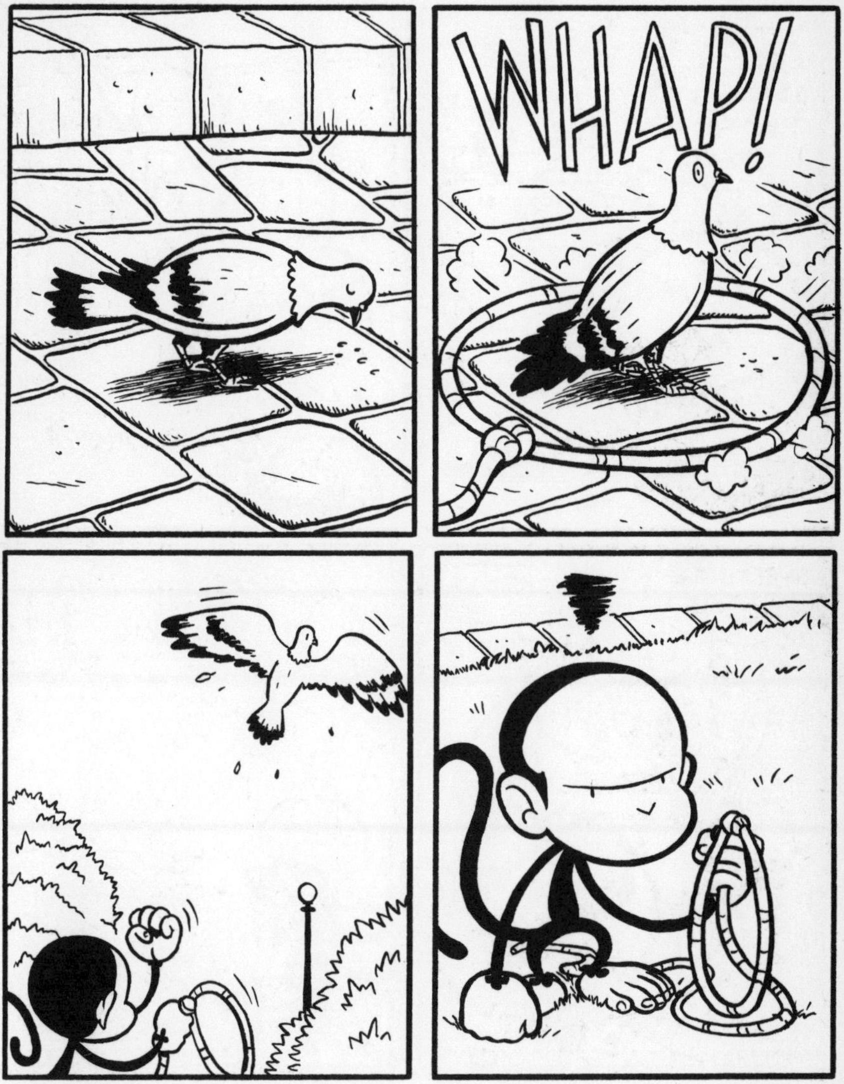
WHAP!

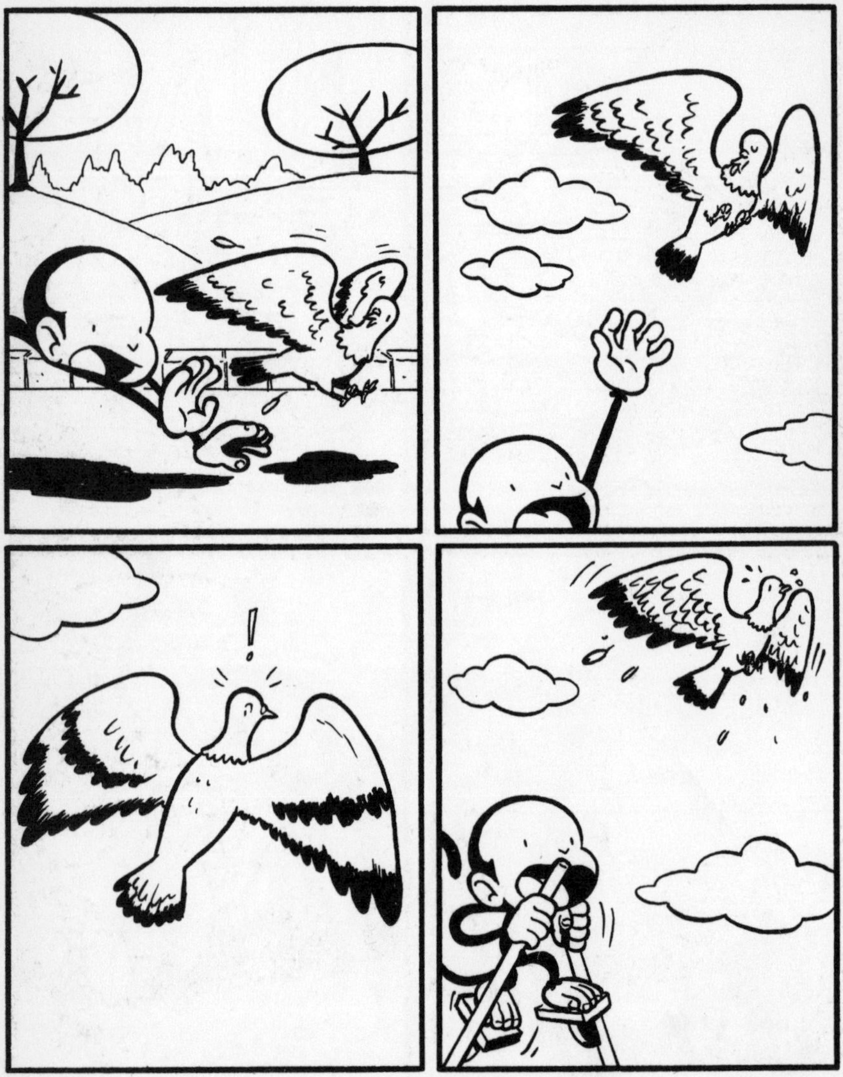
!

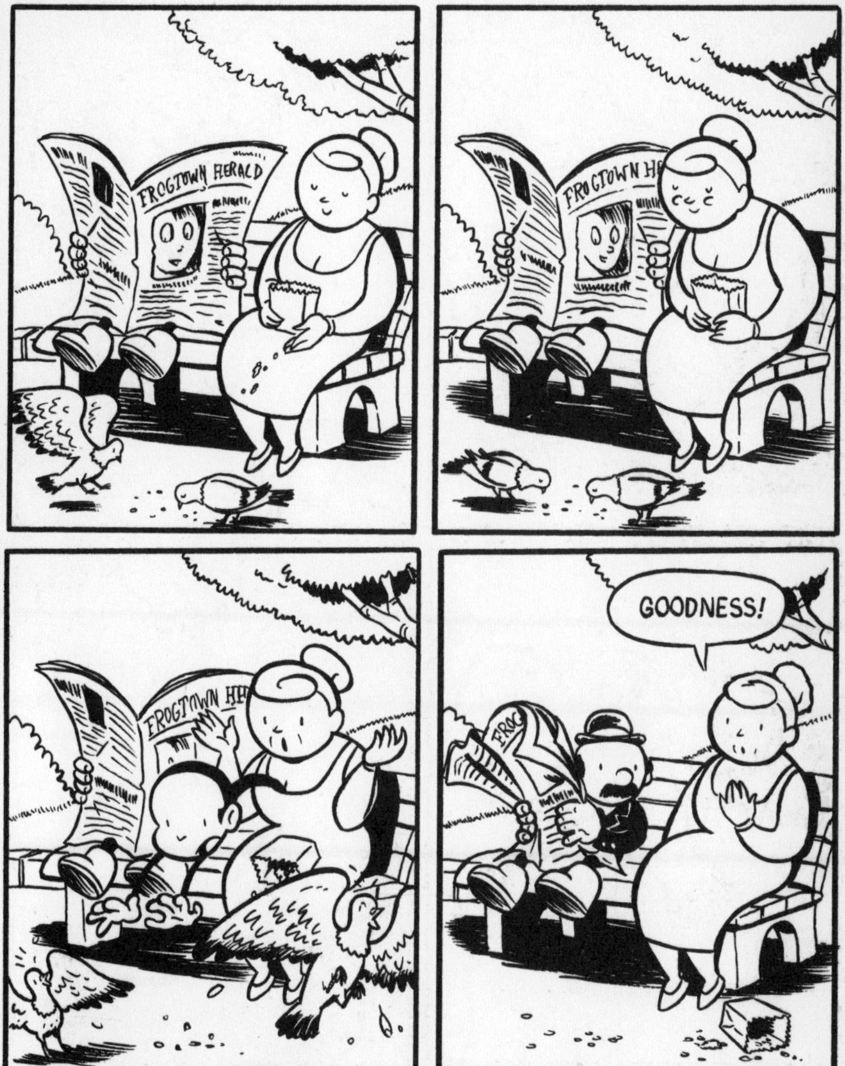

FROGTOWN HERALD
FROGTOWN H
FROGTOWN H
FROG
GOODNESS!

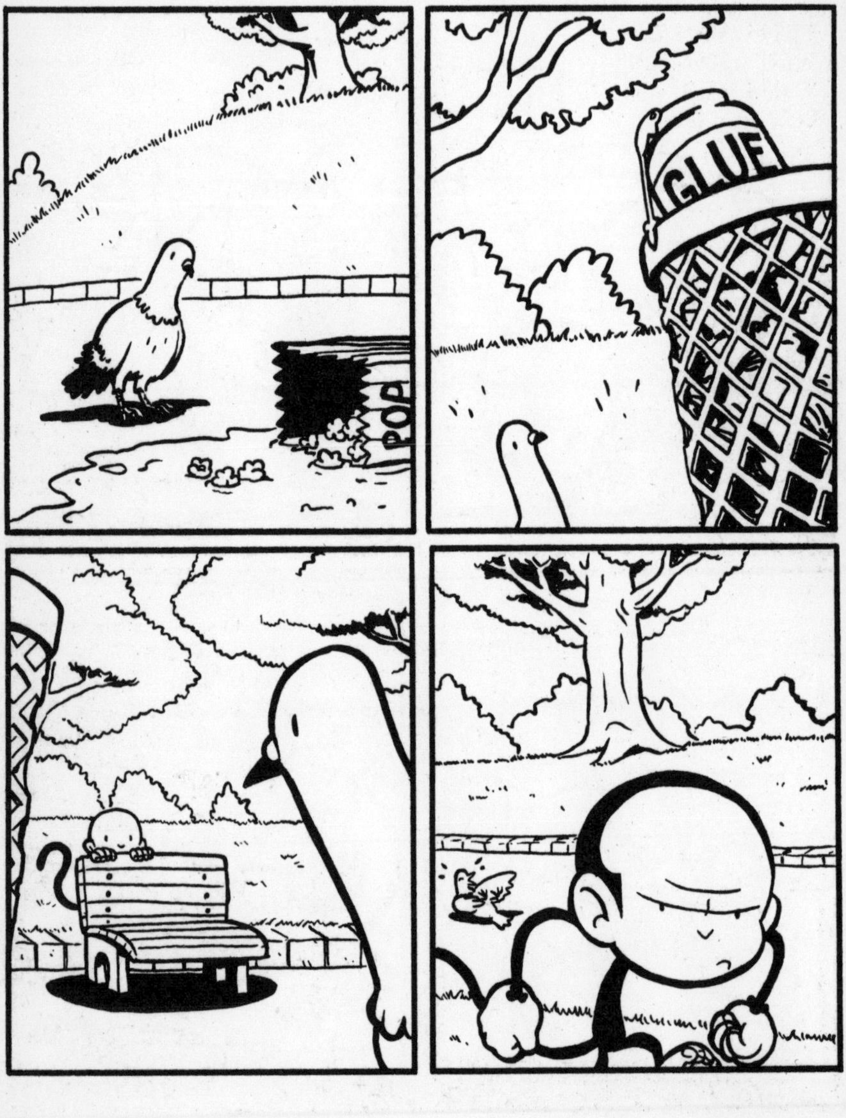
POP
GLUE

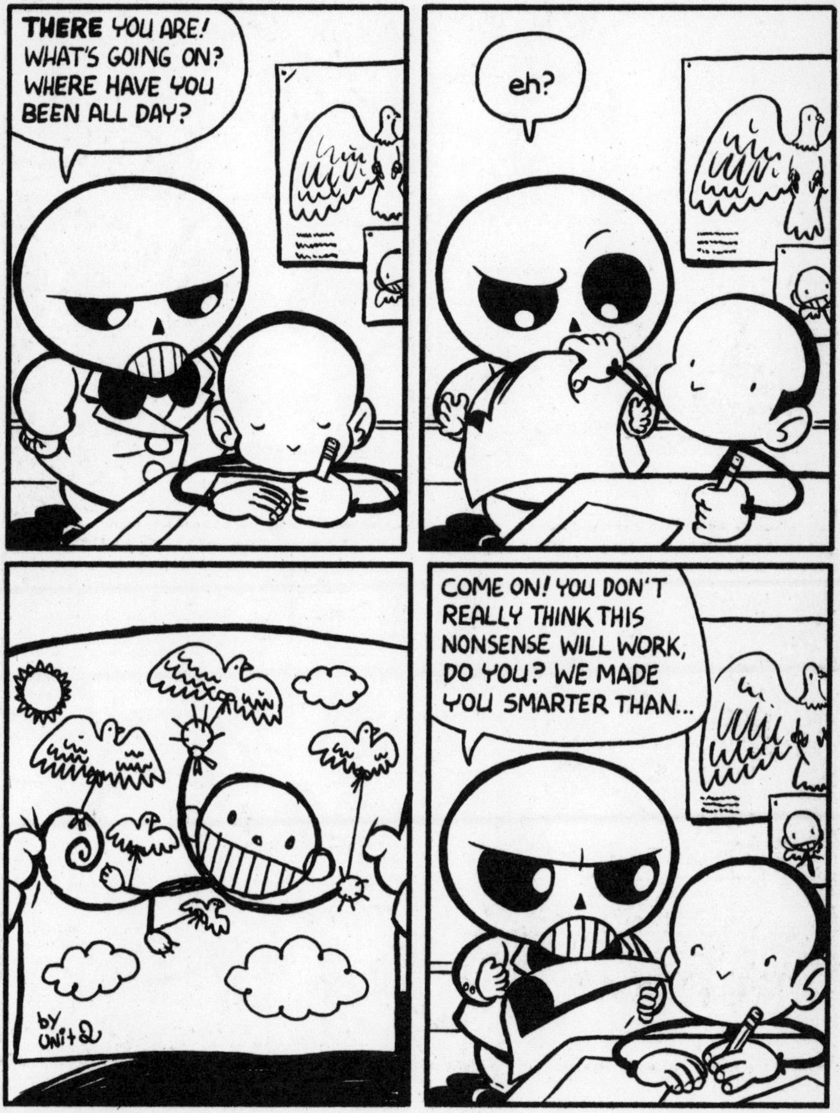
THERE YOU ARE! WHAT'S GOING ON? WHERE HAVE YOU BEEN ALL DAY?
eh?
by UNit2
COME ON! YOU DON'T REALLY THINK THIS NONSENSE WILL WORK, DO YOU? WE MADE YOU SMARTER THAN...

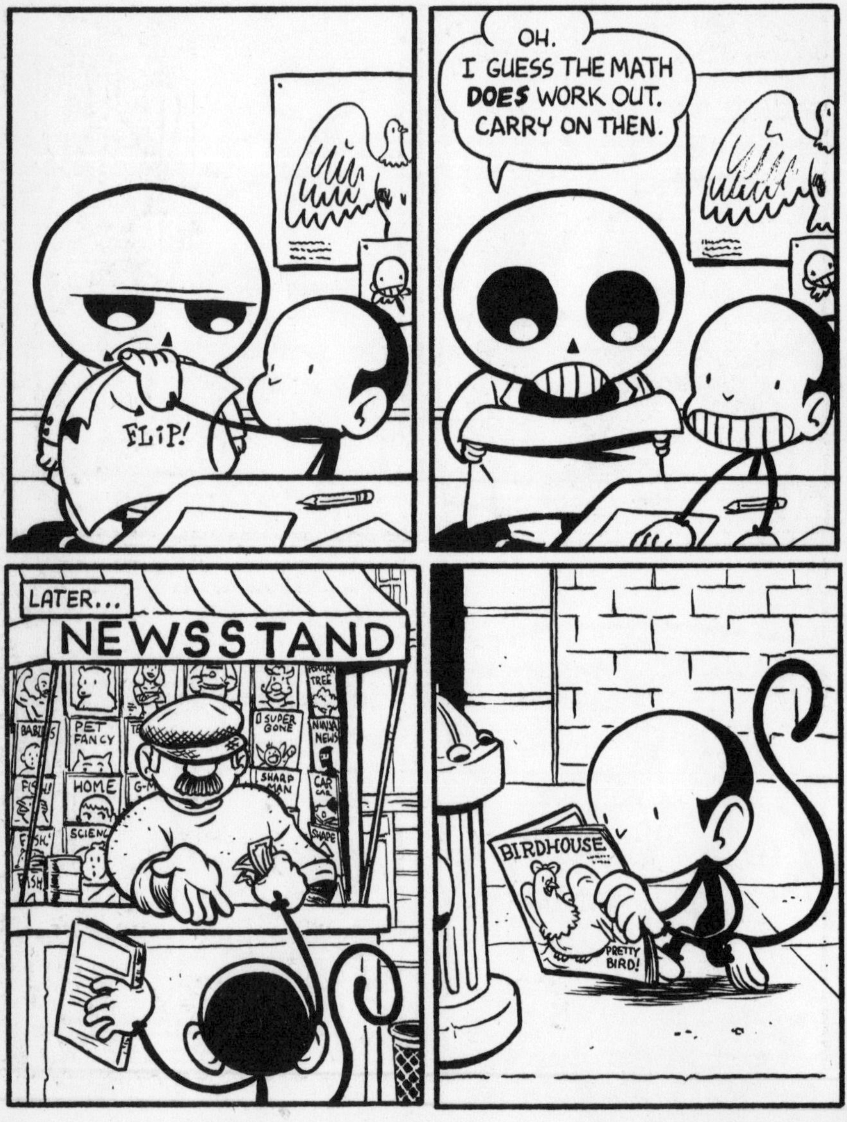
FLIP!
OH.
I GUESS THE MATH
DOES WORK OUT.
CARRY ON THEN.
LATER...
NEWSSTAND
PET FANCY
HOME
SUPER GONE
SHARP MAN
SHAPE
BIRDHOUSE
PRETTY BIRD!

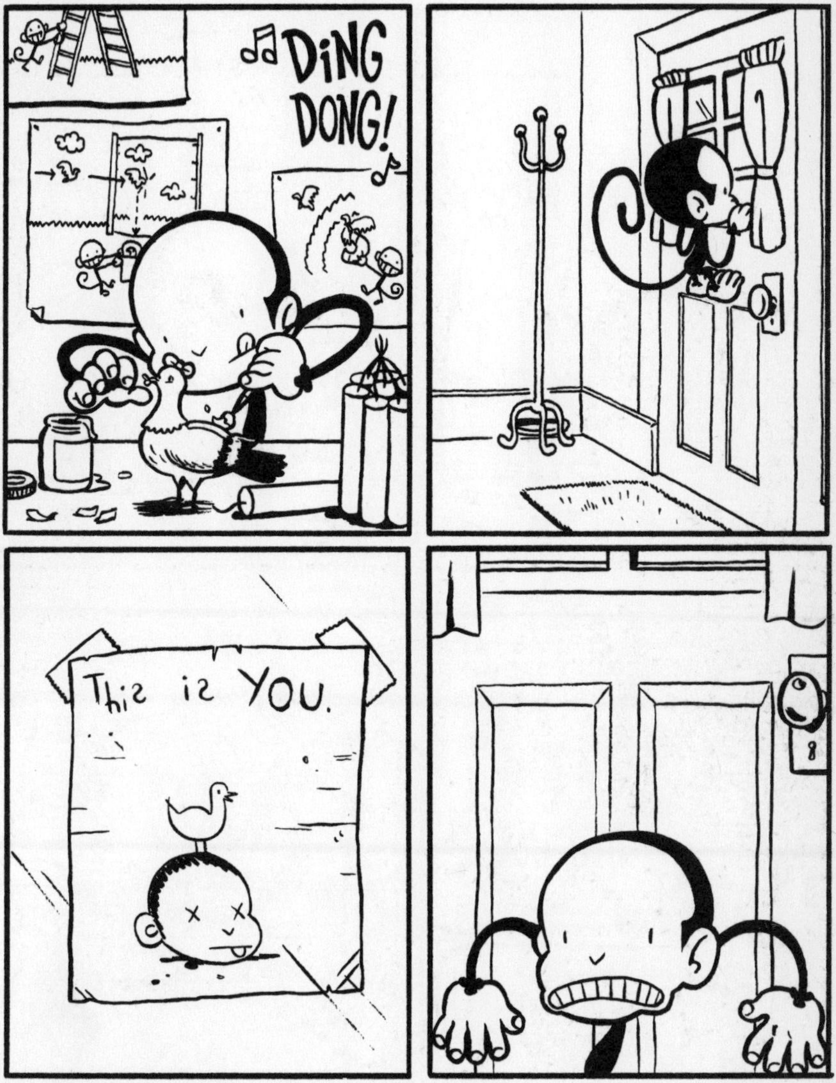
DING DONG!
This is YOU.

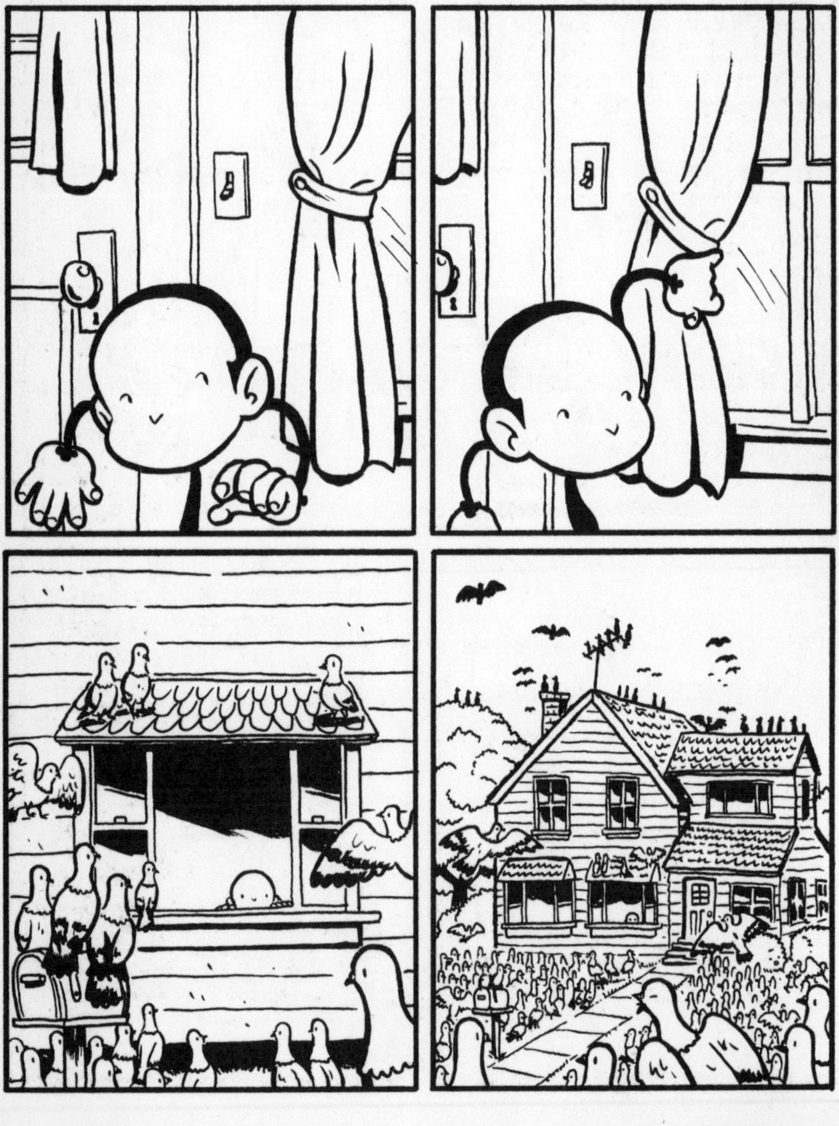

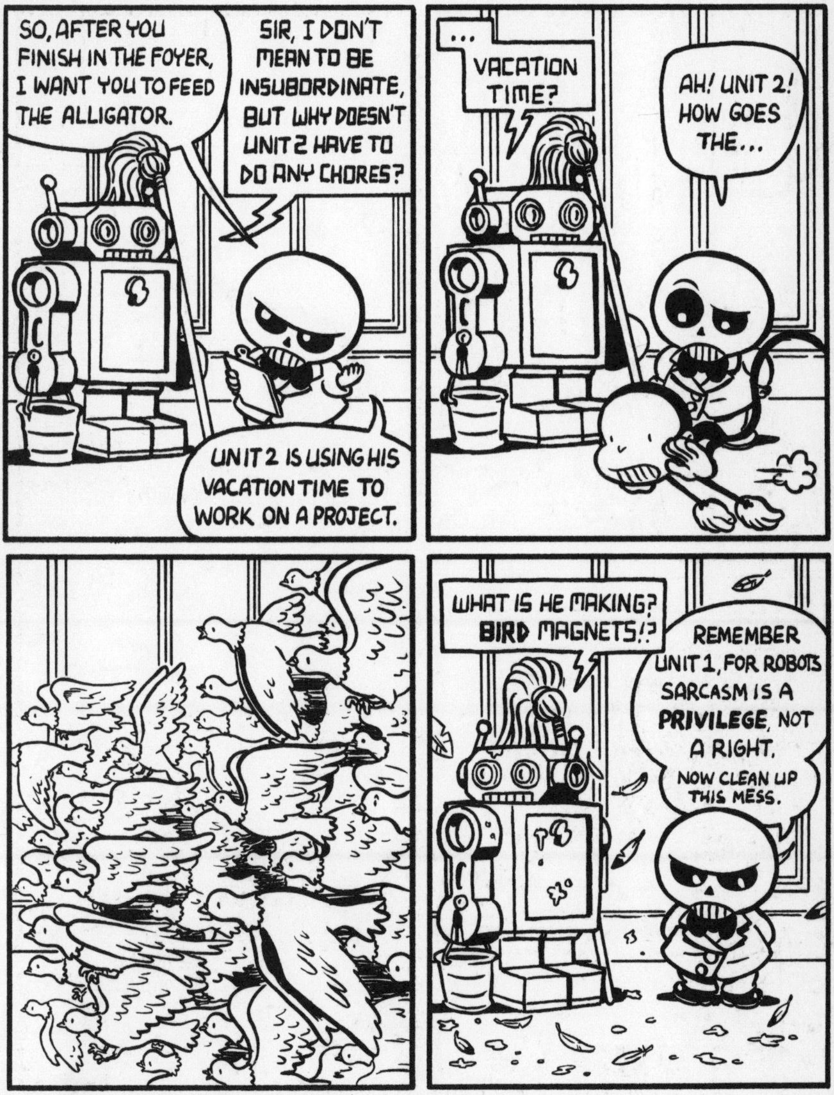
SO, AFTER YOU FINISH IN THE FOYER, I WANT YOU TO FEED THE ALLIGATOR.
SIR, I DON'T MEAN TO BE INSUBORDINATE, BUT WHY DOESN'T UNIT 2 HAVE TO DO ANY CHORES?
UNIT 2 IS USING HIS VACATION TIME TO WORK ON A PROJECT.
...
VACATION TIME?
AH! UNIT 2! HOW GOES THE...
WHAT IS HE MAKING? BIRD MAGNETS!?
REMEMBER UNIT 1, FOR ROBOTS SARCASM IS A PRIVILEGE, NOT A RIGHT.
NOW CLEAN UP THIS MESS.

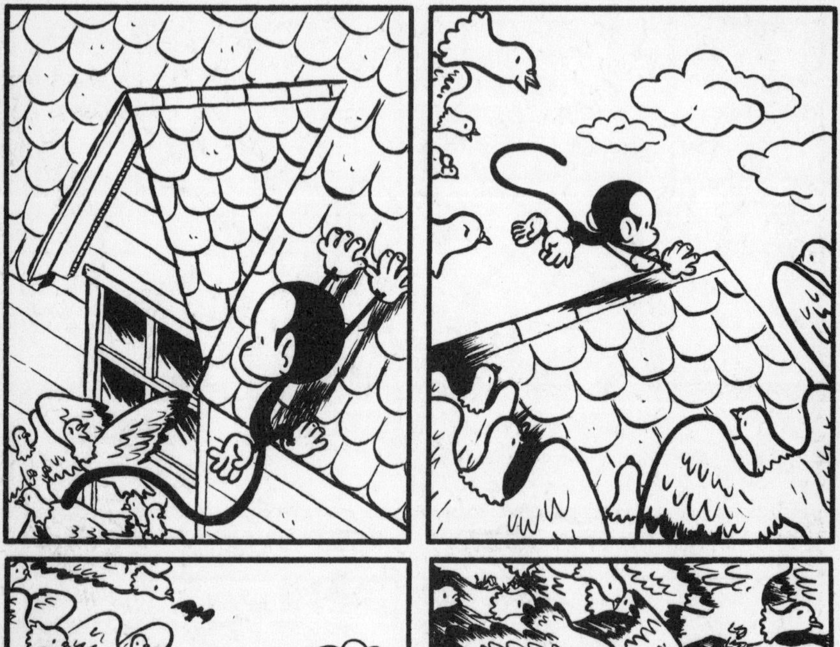
ERT!

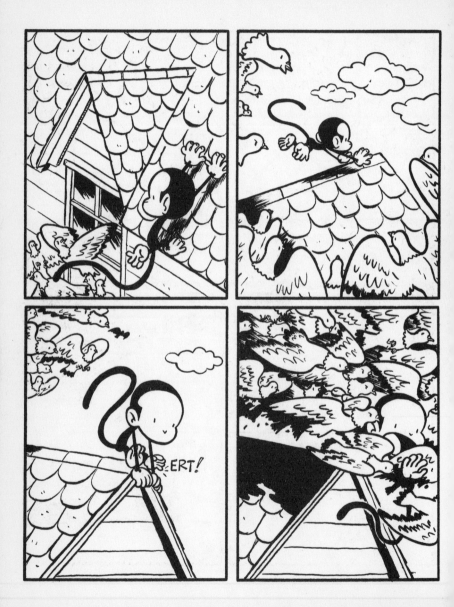

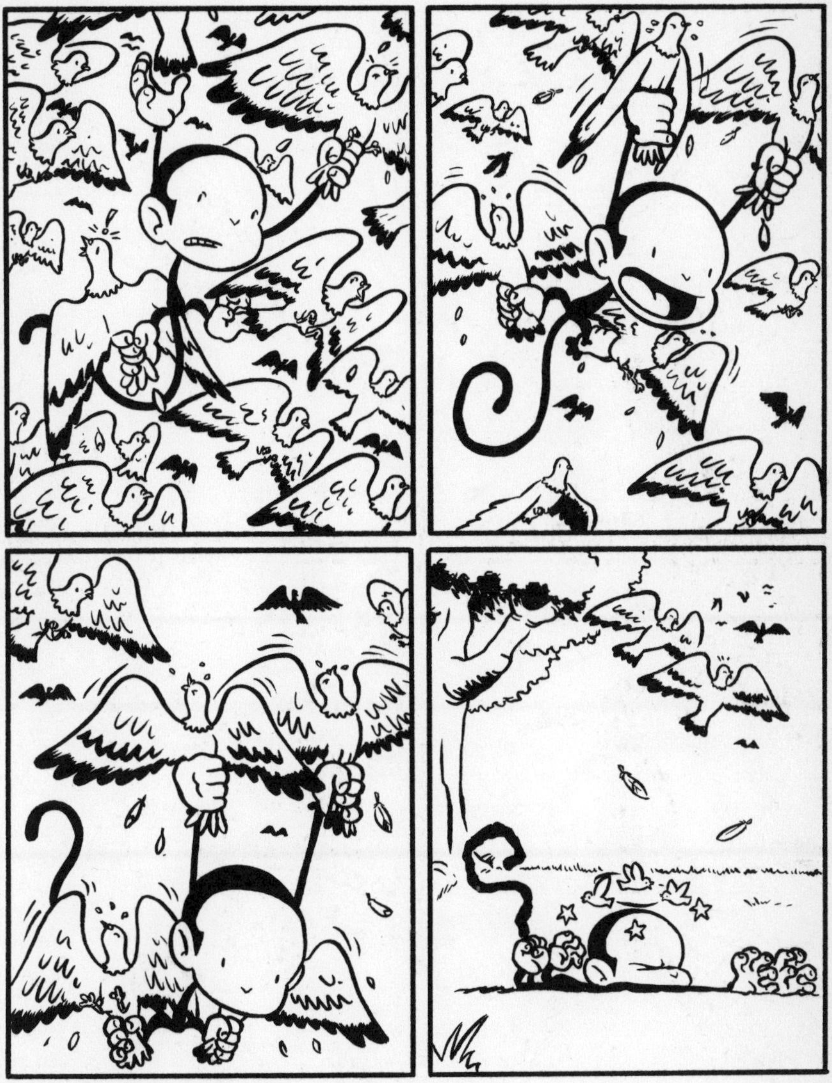

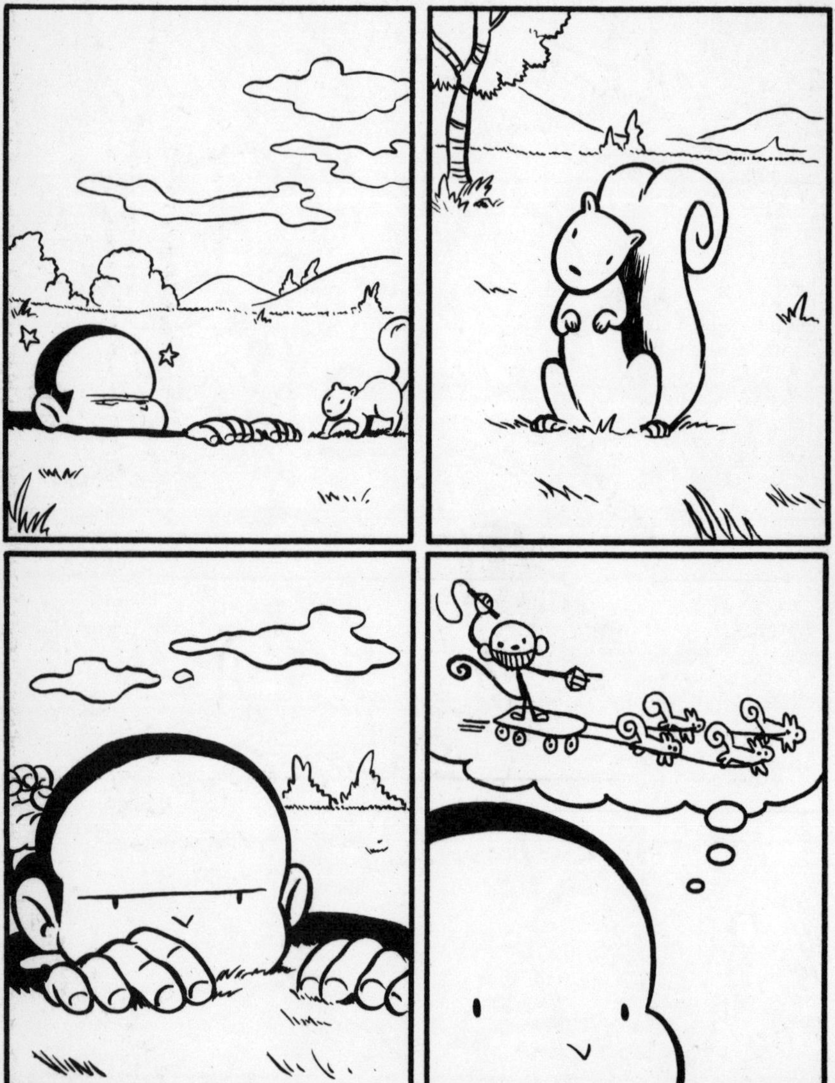

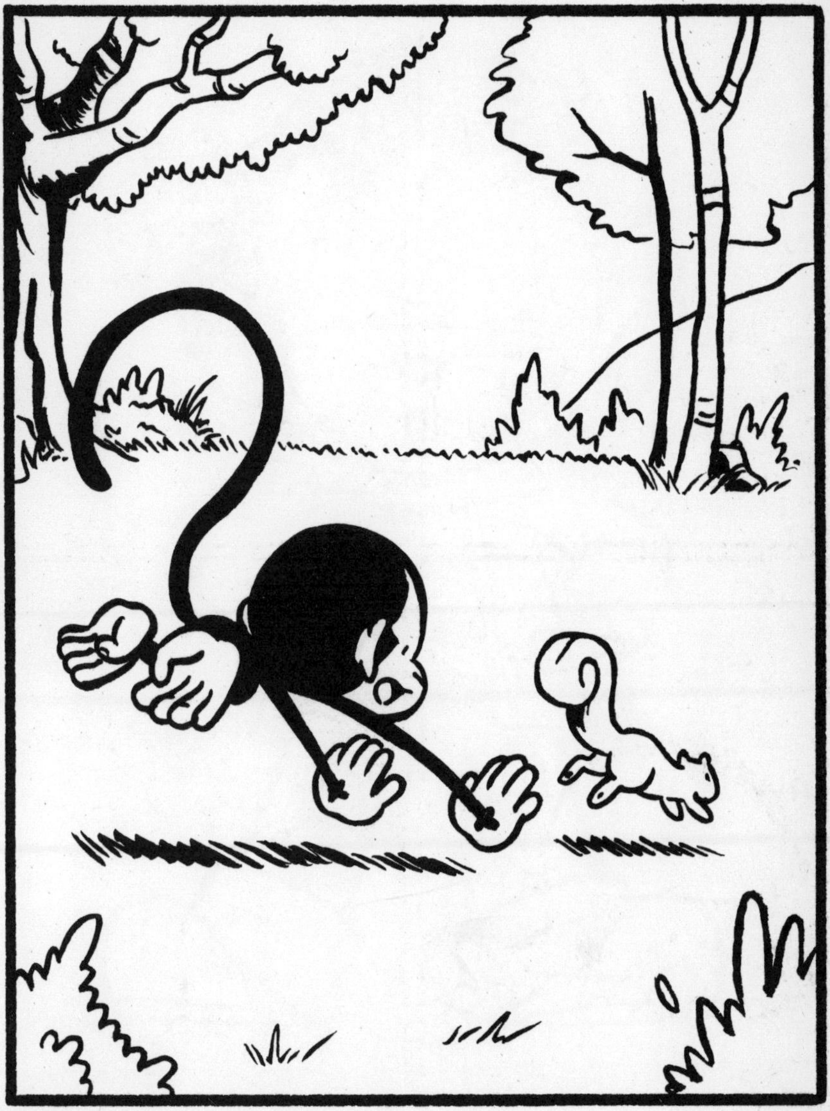

JC·04

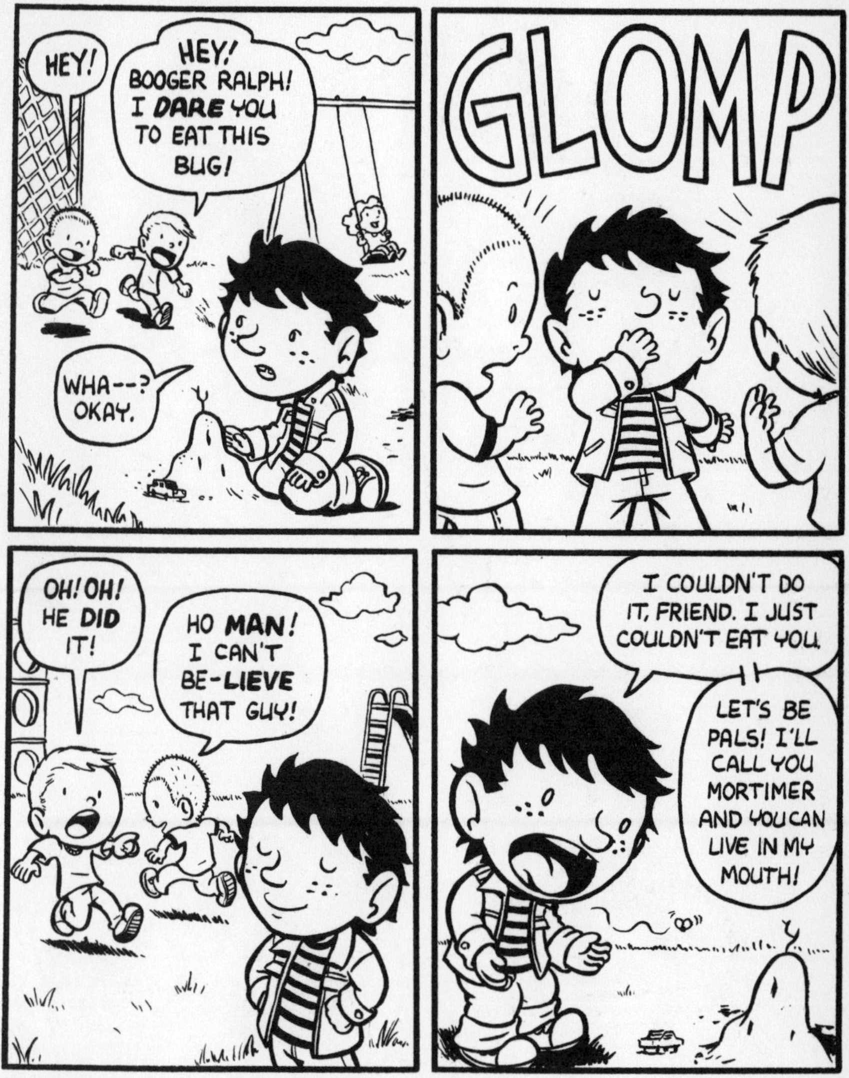
HEY!
HEY! BOOGER RALPH! I DARE YOU TO EAT THIS BUG!
WHA--? OKAY.
GLOMP
OH! OH! HE DID IT!
HO MAN! I CAN'T BE-LIEVE THAT GUY!
I COULDN'T DO IT, FRIEND. I JUST COULDN'T EAT YOU.
LET'S BE PALS! I'LL CALL YOU MORTIMER AND YOU CAN LIVE IN MY MOUTH!

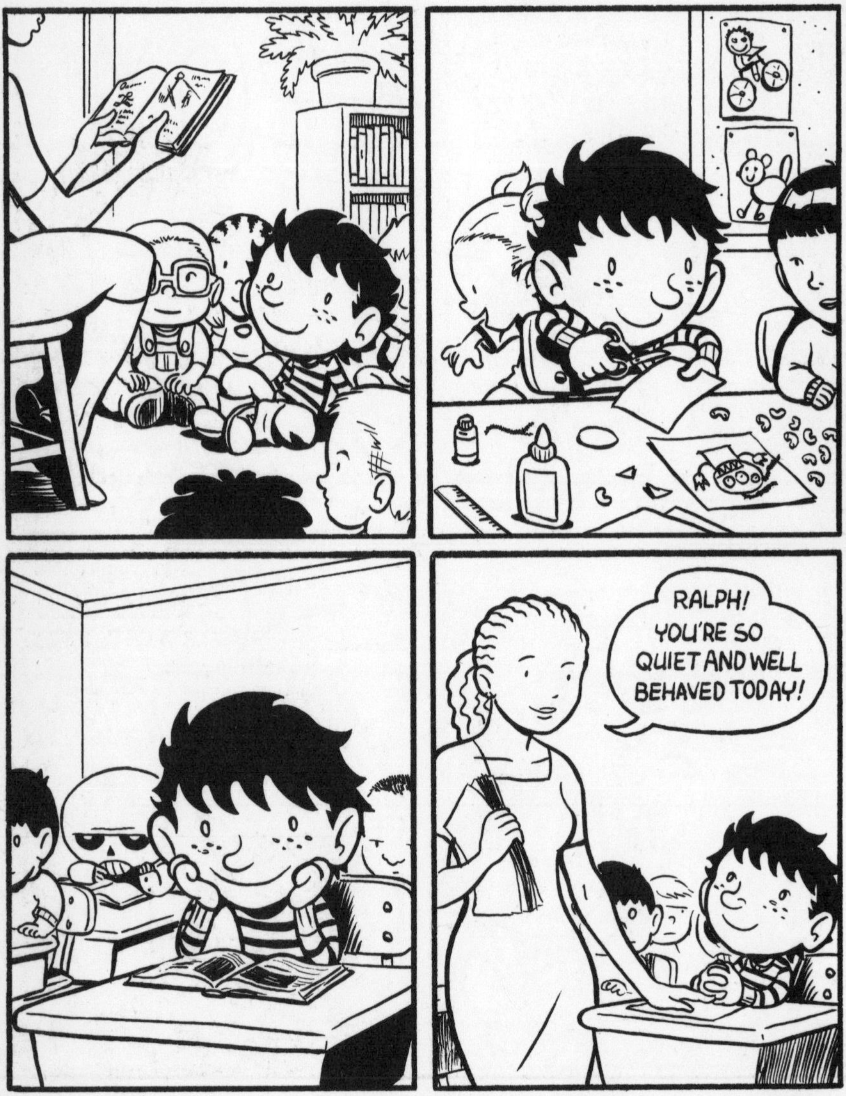
RALPH! YOU'RE SO QUIET AND WELL BEHAVED TODAY!

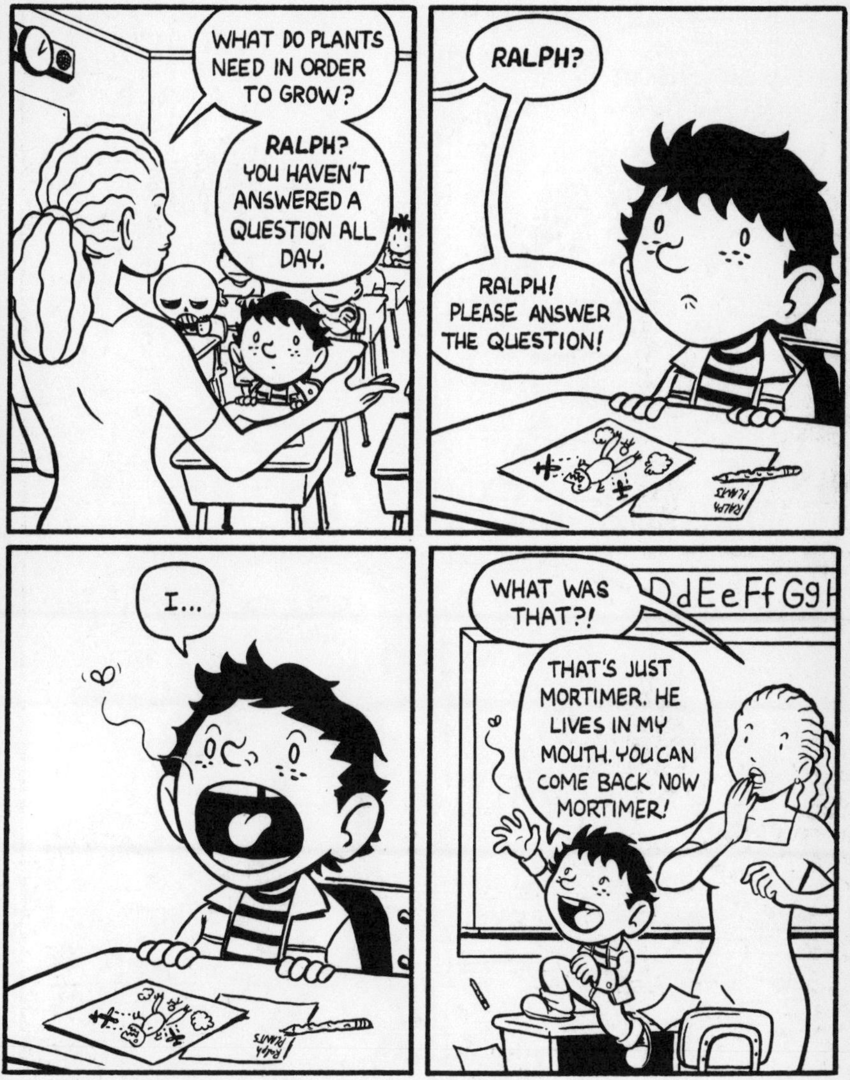
WHAT DO PLANTS NEED IN ORDER TO GROW?
RALPH? YOU HAVEN'T ANSWERED A QUESTION ALL DAY.
RALPH?
RALPH! PLEASE ANSWER THE QUESTION!
RALPH PLANTS
I...
RALPH PLANTS
WHAT WAS THAT?!
DdEeFfGgH
THAT'S JUST MORTIMER. HE LIVES IN MY MOUTH. YOU CAN COME BACK NOW MORTIMER!

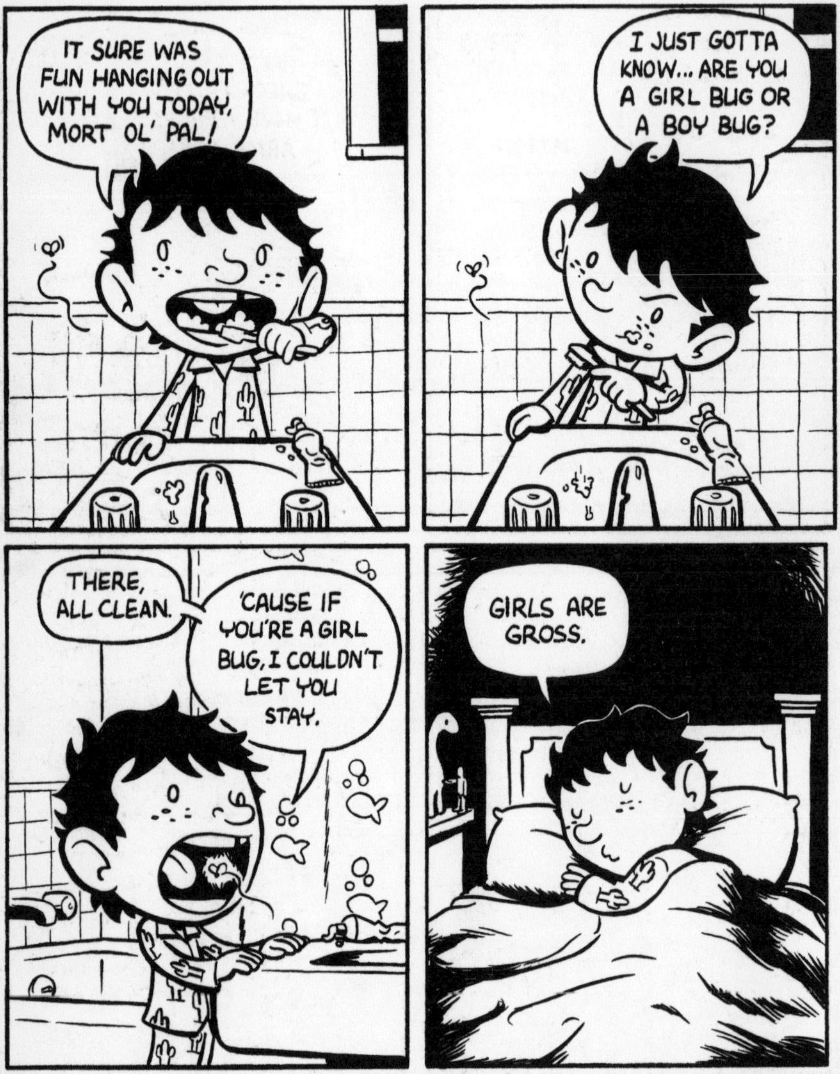
IT SURE WAS FUN HANGING OUT WITH YOU TODAY, MORT OL' PAL!
I JUST GOTTA KNOW... ARE YOU A GIRL BUG OR A BOY BUG?
THERE, ALL CLEAN.
'CAUSE IF YOU'RE A GIRL BUG, I COULDN'T LET YOU STAY.
GIRLS ARE GROSS.

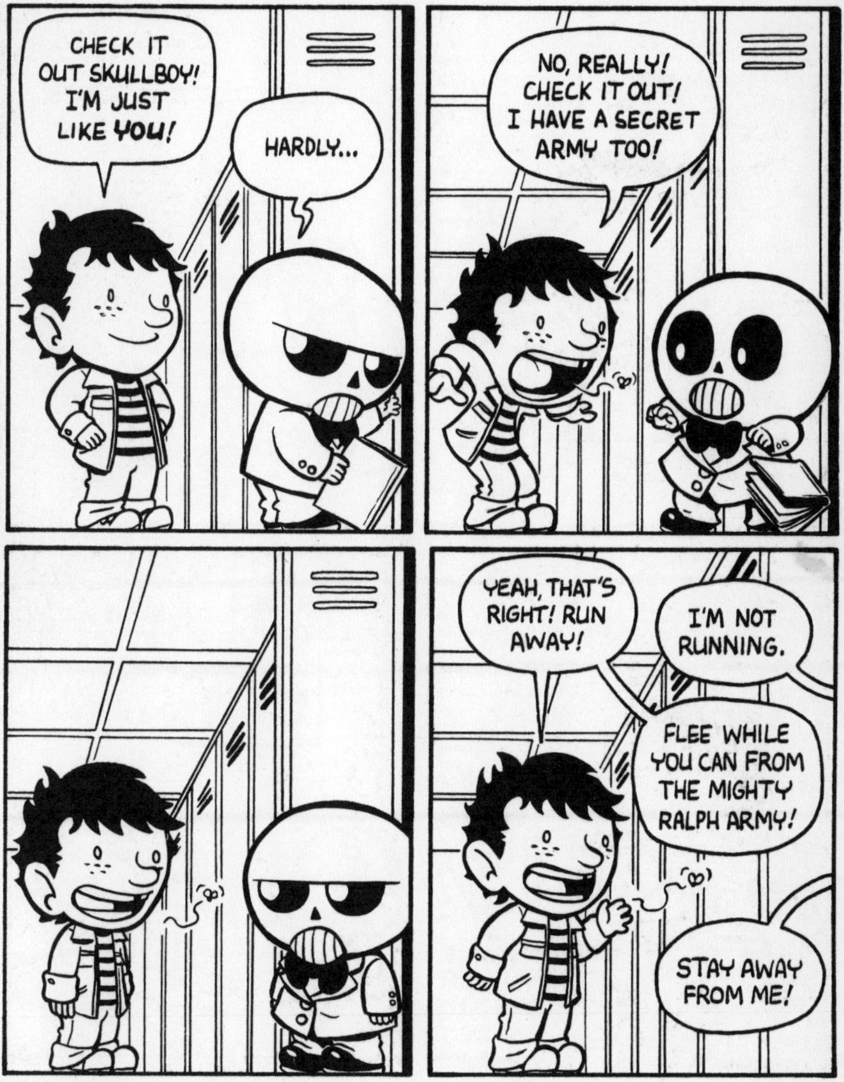
CHECK IT OUT SKULLBOY! I'M JUST LIKE YOU!
HARDLY...
NO, REALLY! CHECK IT OUT! I HAVE A SECRET ARMY TOO!
YEAH, THAT'S RIGHT! RUN AWAY!
I'M NOT RUNNING.
FLEE WHILE YOU CAN FROM THE MIGHTY RALPH ARMY!
STAY AWAY FROM ME!

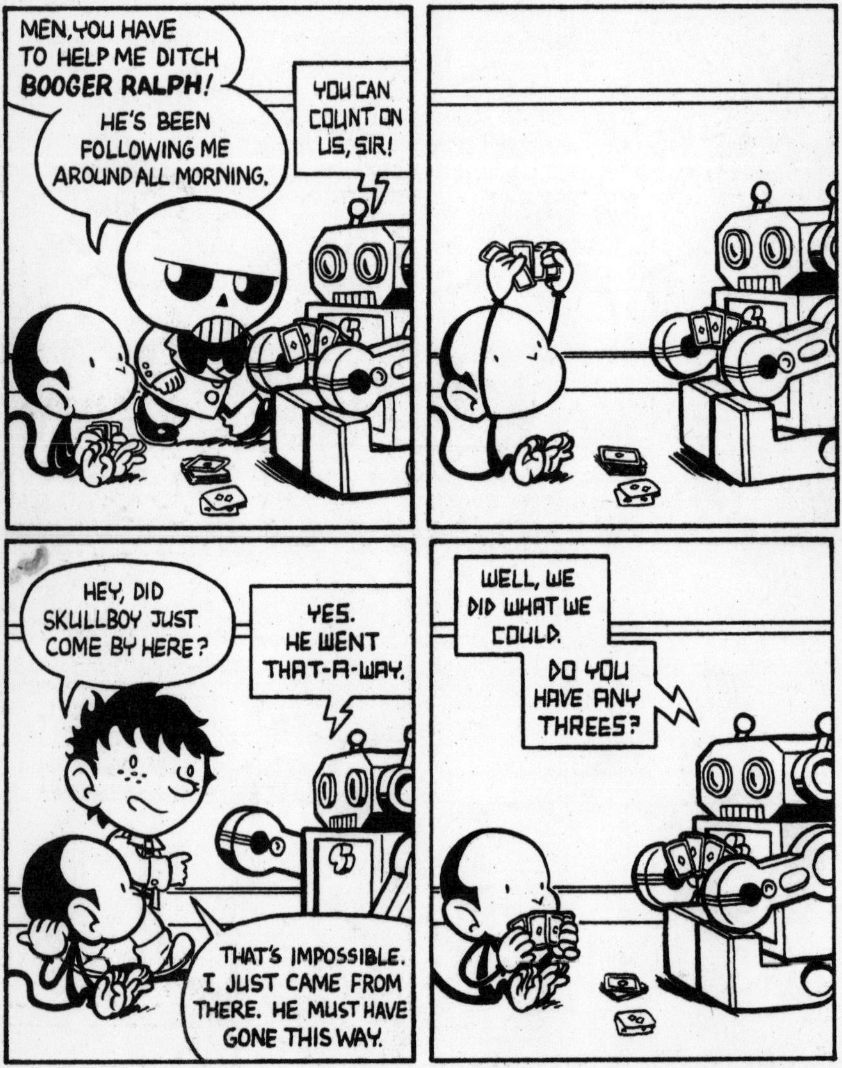
MEN, YOU HAVE TO HELP ME DITCH BOOGER RALPH!
HE'S BEEN FOLLOWING ME AROUND ALL MORNING.
YOU CAN COUNT ON US, SIR!
HEY, DID SKULLBOY JUST COME BY HERE?
YES. HE WENT THAT-A-WAY.
THAT'S IMPOSSIBLE. I JUST CAME FROM THERE. HE MUST HAVE GONE THIS WAY.
WELL, WE DID WHAT WE COULD.
DO YOU HAVE ANY THREES?

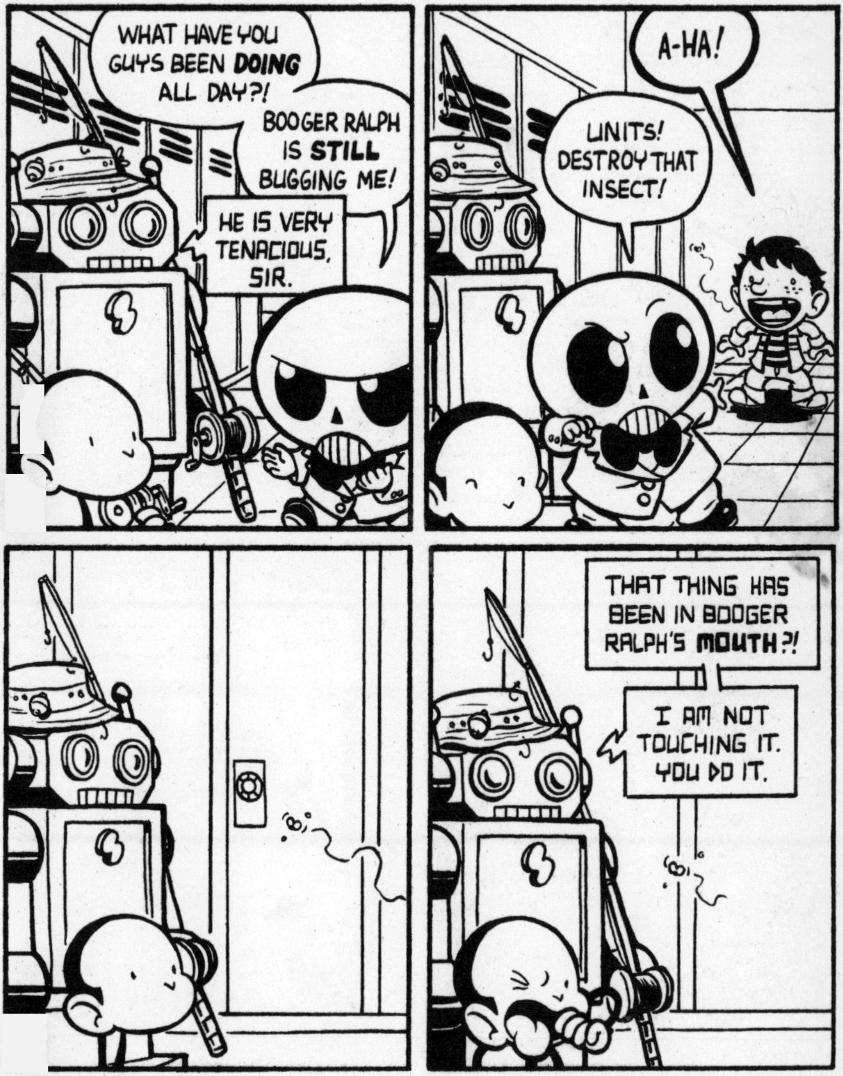
WHAT HAVE YOU GUYS BEEN **DOING** ALL DAY?!
BOOGER RALPH IS **STILL** BUGGING ME!
HE IS VERY TENACIOUS, SIR.
A-HA!
UNITS! DESTROY THAT INSECT!
THAT THING HAS BEEN IN BOOGER RALPH'S **MOUTH**?!
I AM NOT TOUCHING IT. YOU DO IT.

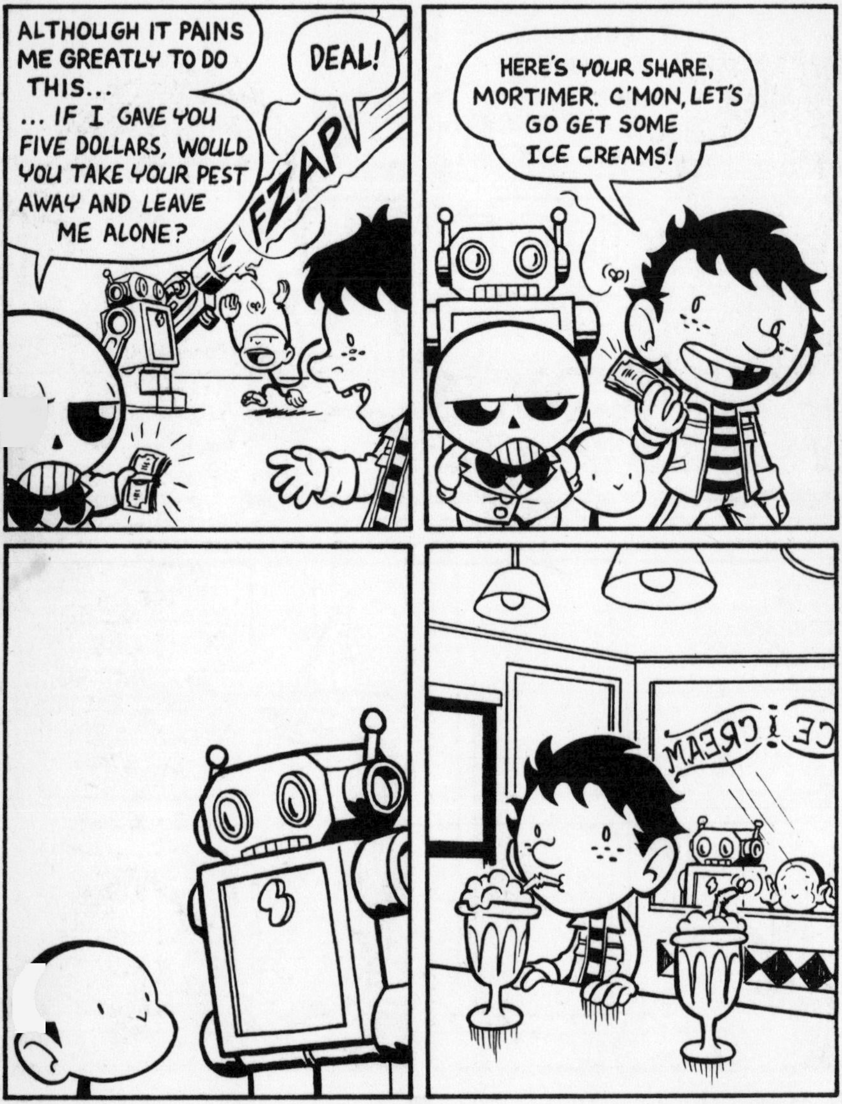
ALTHOUGH IT PAINS ME GREATLY TO DO THIS... ... IF I GAVE YOU FIVE DOLLARS, WOULD YOU TAKE YOUR PEST AWAY AND LEAVE ME ALONE?
DEAL!
FZAP
HERE'S YOUR SHARE, MORTIMER. C'MON, LET'S GO GET SOME ICE CREAMS!
ICE CREAM

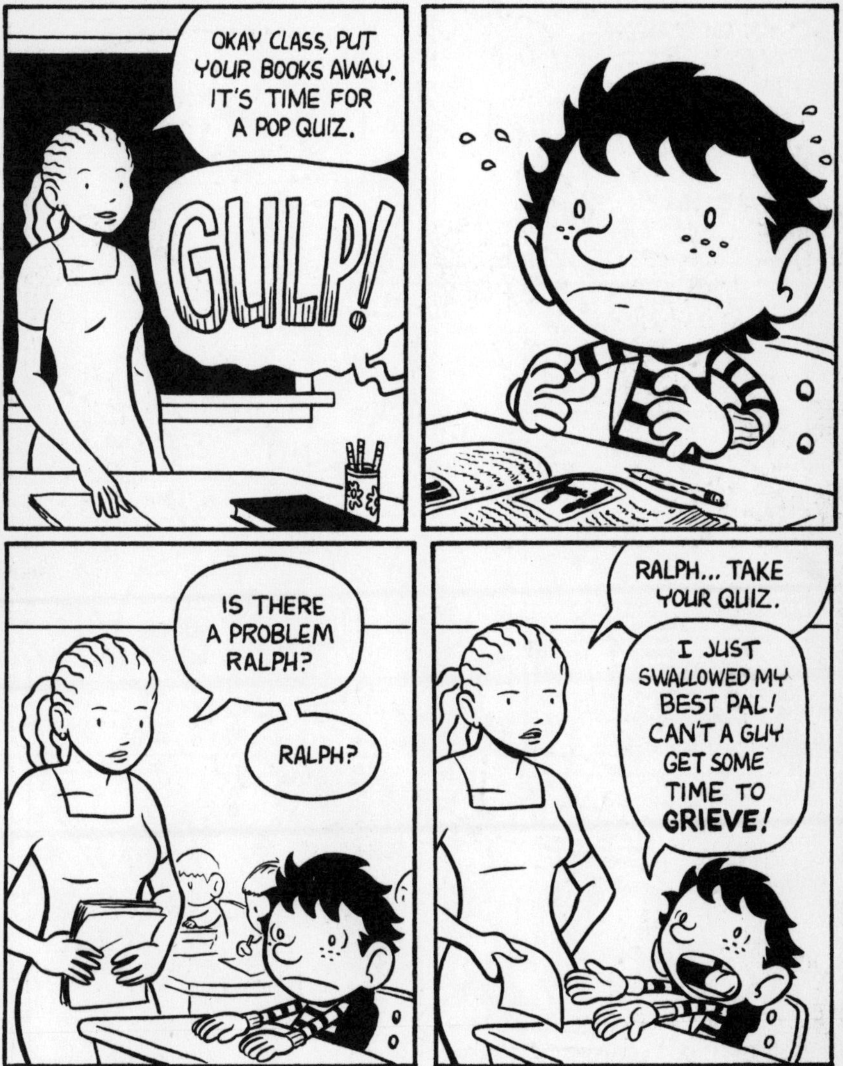
OKAY CLASS, PUT YOUR BOOKS AWAY. IT'S TIME FOR A POP QUIZ.
GULP!
IS THERE A PROBLEM RALPH?
RALPH?
RALPH... TAKE YOUR QUIZ.
I JUST SWALLOWED MY BEST PAL! CAN'T A GUY GET SOME TIME TO GRIEVE!
JC· 04

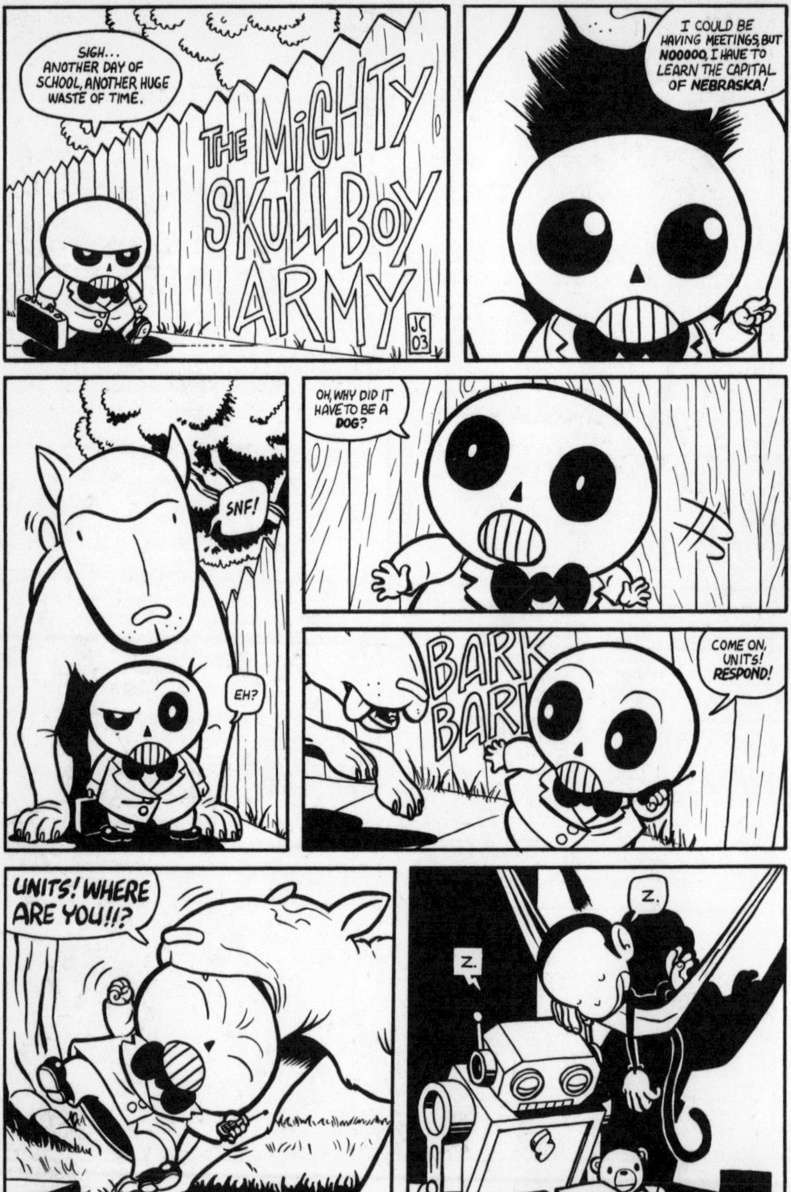

SIGH... ANOTHER DAY OF SCHOOL, ANOTHER HUGE WASTE OF TIME.
THE MIGHTY SKULLBOY ARMY
JC 03
I COULD BE HAVING MEETINGS, BUT NOOOOO, I HAVE TO LEARN THE CAPITAL OF NEBRASKA!
SNF!
EH?
OH, WHY DID IT HAVE TO BE A DOG?
BARK BARK
COME ON, UNITS! RESPOND!
UNITS! WHERE ARE YOU!!?
Z.
Z.

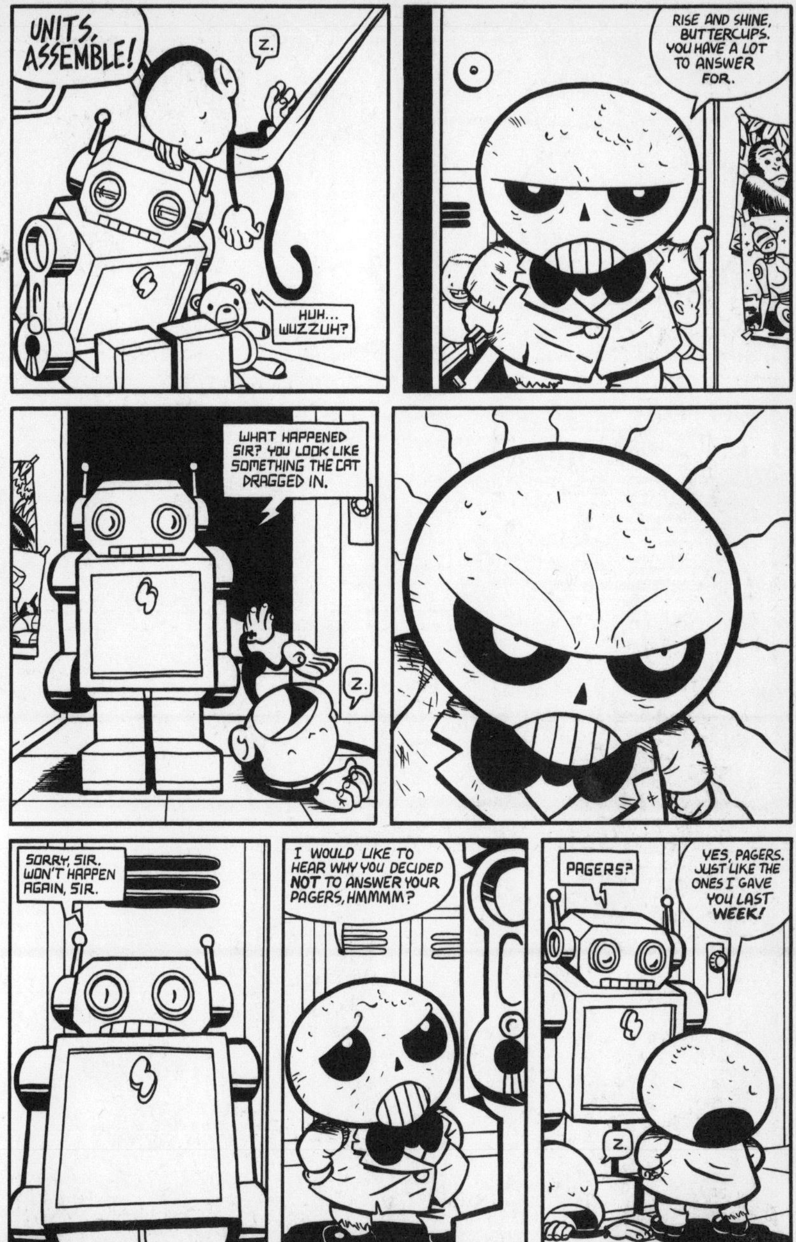
UNITS, ASSEMBLE!
Z.
HUH... WUZZUH?
RISE AND SHINE, BUTTERCUPS. YOU HAVE A LOT TO ANSWER FOR.
WHAT HAPPENED SIR? YOU LOOK LIKE SOMETHING THE CAT DRAGGED IN.
Z.
SORRY, SIR. WON'T HAPPEN AGAIN, SIR.
I WOULD LIKE TO HEAR WHY YOU DECIDED NOT TO ANSWER YOUR PAGERS, HMMMM?
PAGERS?
YES, PAGERS. JUST LIKE THE ONES I GAVE YOU LAST WEEK!
Z.

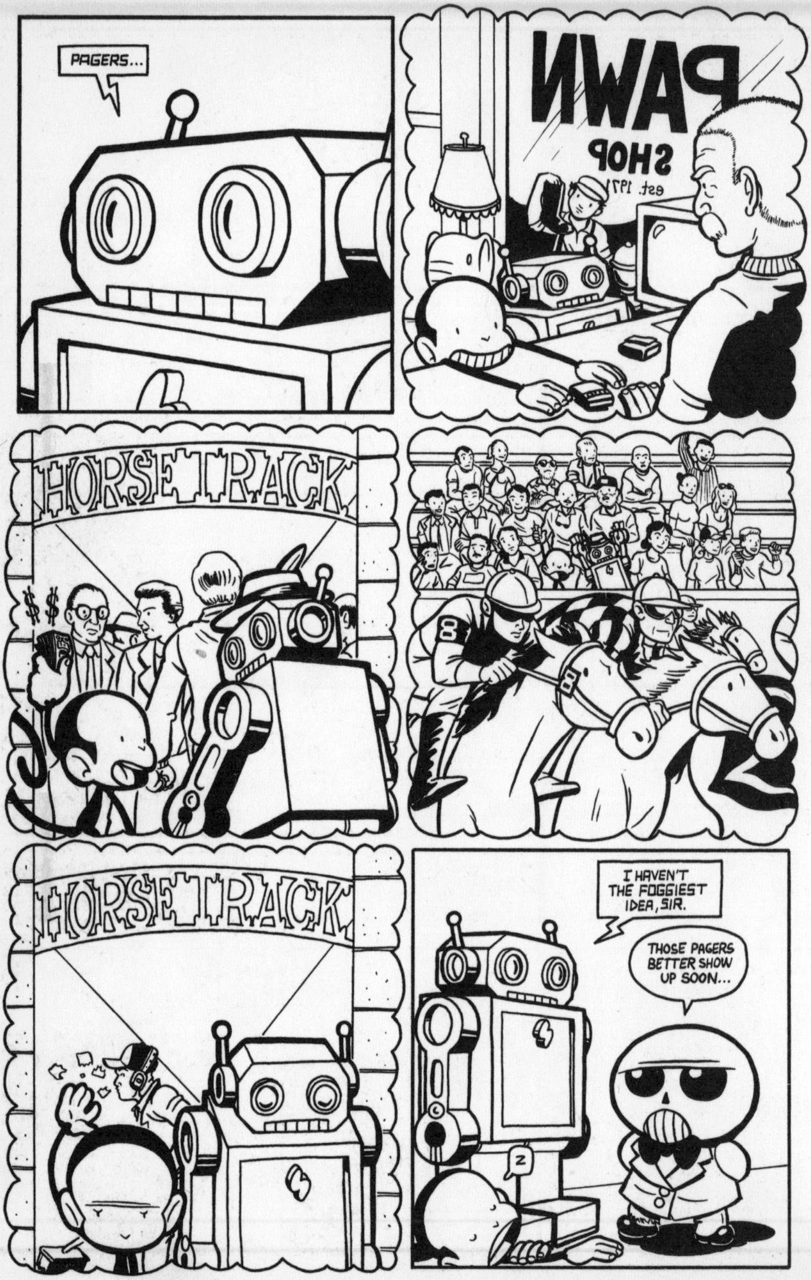
PAGERS...
PAWN
SHOP
est. 1971
HORSE TRACK
HORSE TRACK
I HAVEN'T THE FOGGIEST IDEA, SIR.
THOSE PAGERS BETTER SHOW UP SOON...
Z

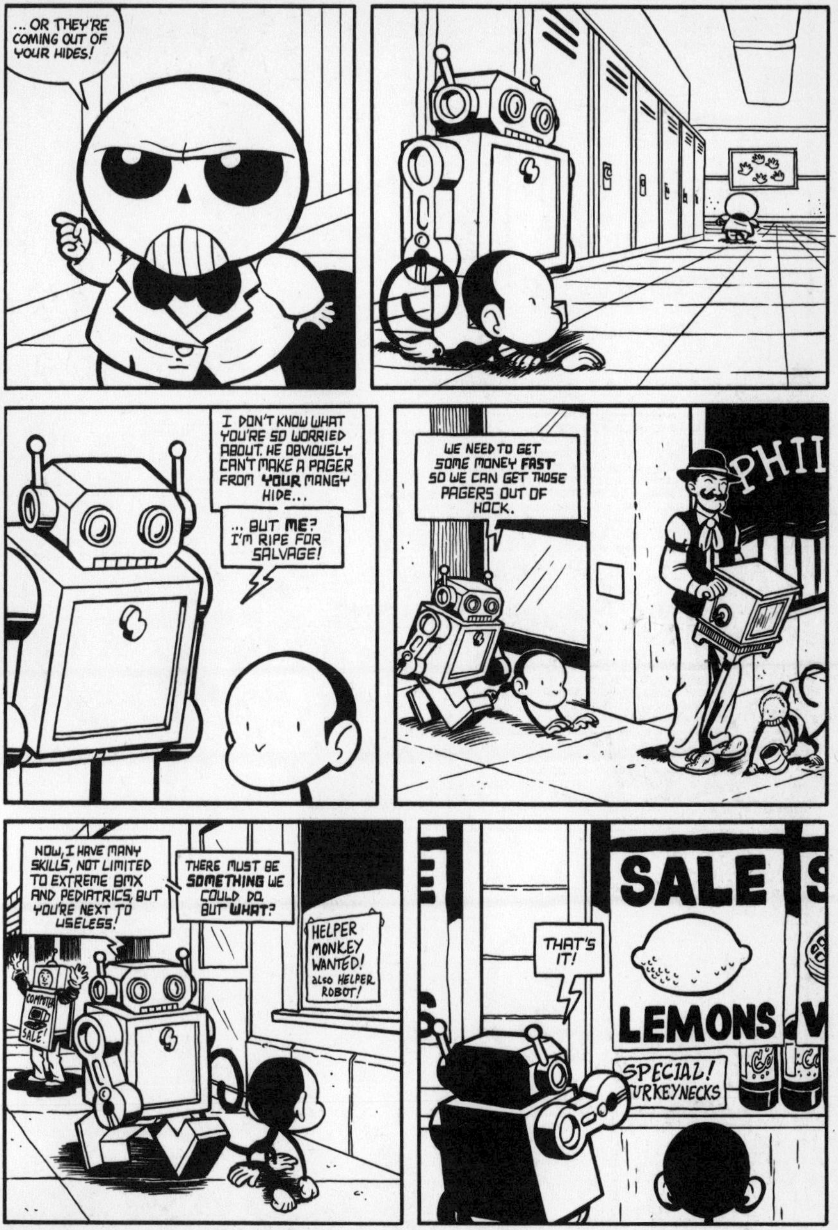
... OR THEY'RE COMING OUT OF YOUR HIDES!
I DON'T KNOW WHAT YOU'RE SO WORRIED ABOUT. HE OBVIOUSLY CAN'T MAKE A PAGER FROM YOUR MANGY HIDE...
... BUT ME? I'M RIPE FOR SALVAGE!
WE NEED TO GET SOME MONEY FAST SO WE CAN GET THOSE PAGERS OUT OF HOCK.
PHII
NOW, I HAVE MANY SKILLS, NOT LIMITED TO EXTREME BMX AND PEDIATRICS, BUT YOU'RE NEXT TO USELESS!
THERE MUST BE SOMETHING WE COULD DO. BUT WHAT?
HELPER MONKEY WANTED! also HELPER ROBOT!
COMPUTER SALE!
SALE
LEMONS
SPECIAL! TURKEYNECKS
THAT'S IT!

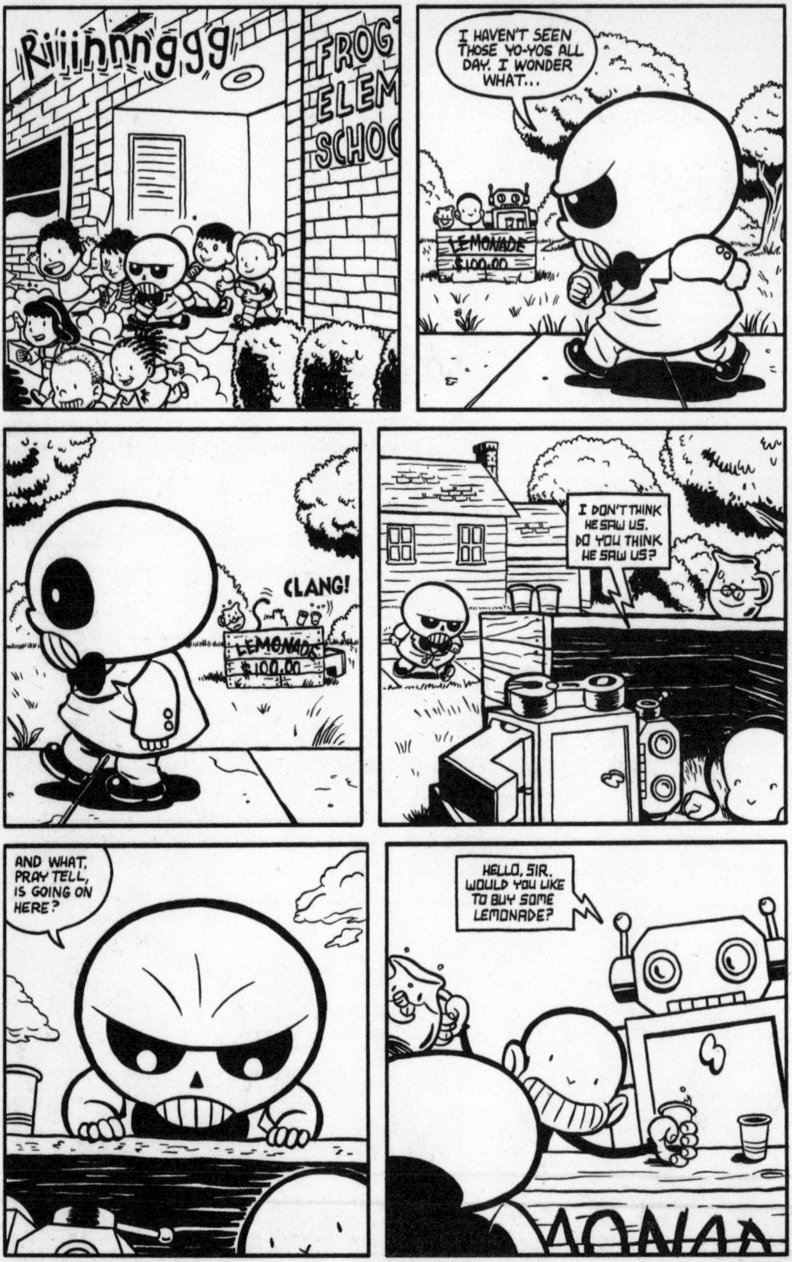
Riiinnnggg
FROG ELEM SCHOO
I HAVEN'T SEEN THOSE YO-YOS ALL DAY. I WONDER WHAT...
LEMONADE $100.00
CLANG!
LEMONADE $100.00
I DON'T THINK HE SAW US. DO YOU THINK HE SAW US?
AND WHAT, PRAY TELL, IS GOING ON HERE?
HELLO, SIR. WOULD YOU LIKE TO BUY SOME LEMONADE?

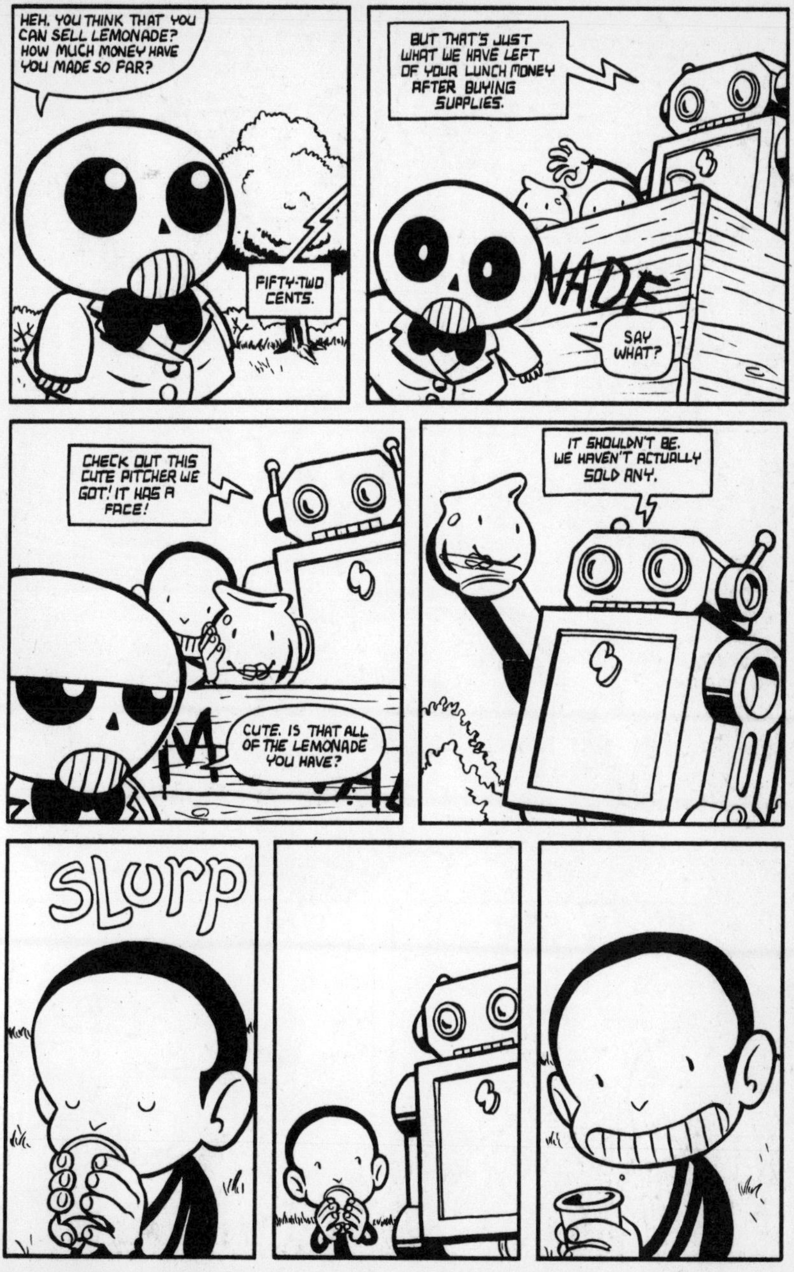
HEH. YOU THINK THAT YOU CAN SELL LEMONADE? HOW MUCH MONEY HAVE YOU MADE SO FAR?
FIFTY-TWO CENTS.
BUT THAT'S JUST WHAT WE HAVE LEFT OF YOUR LUNCH MONEY AFTER BUYING SUPPLIES.
NADE
SAY WHAT?
CHECK OUT THIS CUTE PITCHER WE GOT! IT HAS A FACE!
CUTE. IS THAT ALL OF THE LEMONADE YOU HAVE?
IT SHOULDN'T BE. WE HAVEN'T ACTUALLY SOLD ANY.
SLURP

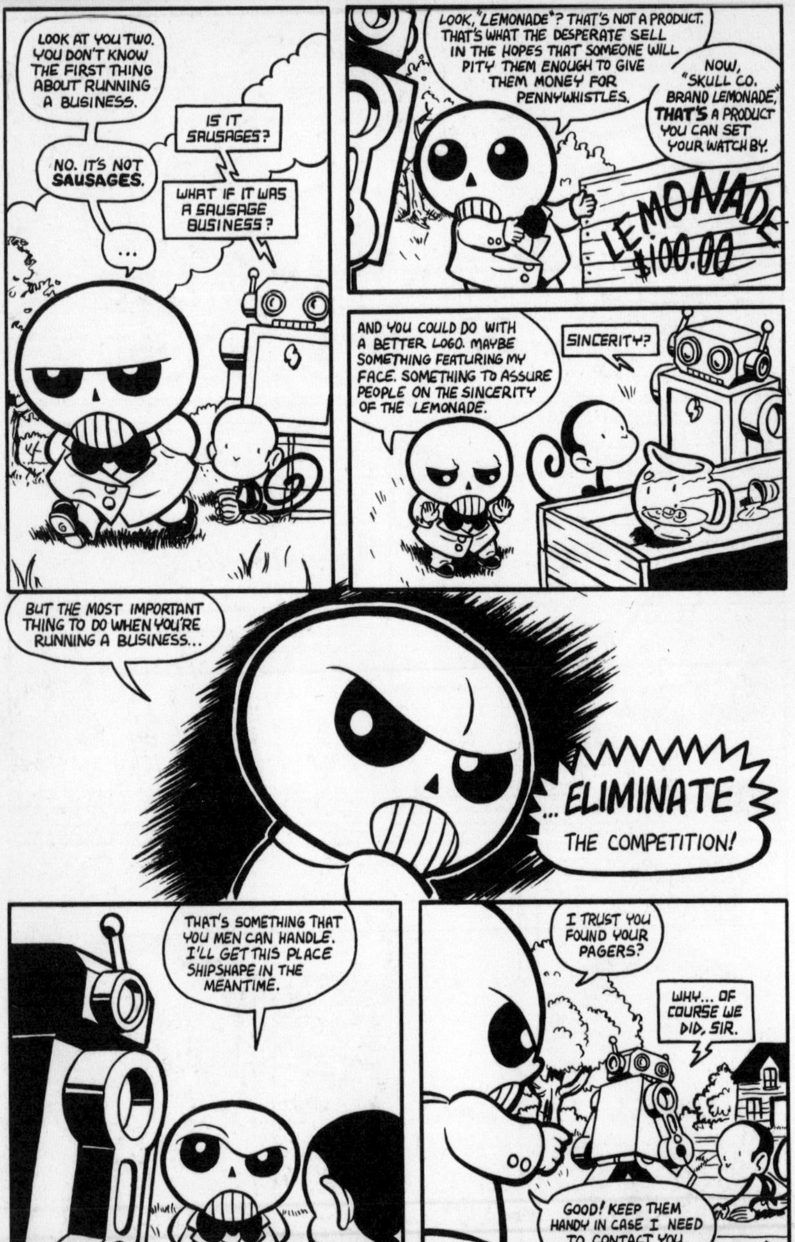
LOOK AT YOU TWO. YOU DON'T KNOW THE FIRST THING ABOUT RUNNING A BUSINESS.
IS IT SAUSAGES?
NO. IT'S NOT **SAUSAGES**.
WHAT IF IT WAS A SAUSAGE BUSINESS?
...
LOOK, "LEMONADE"? THAT'S NOT A PRODUCT. THAT'S WHAT THE DESPERATE SELL IN THE HOPES THAT SOMEONE WILL PITY THEM ENOUGH TO GIVE THEM MONEY FOR PENNYWHISTLES.
NOW, "SKULL CO. BRAND LEMONADE," **THAT'S** A PRODUCT YOU CAN SET YOUR WATCH BY.
LEMONADE
$100.00
AND YOU COULD DO WITH A BETTER LOGO. MAYBE SOMETHING FEATURING MY FACE. SOMETHING TO ASSURE PEOPLE ON THE SINCERITY OF THE LEMONADE.
SINCERITY?
BUT THE MOST IMPORTANT THING TO DO WHEN YOU'RE RUNNING A BUSINESS...
...ELIMINATE THE COMPETITION!
THAT'S SOMETHING THAT YOU MEN CAN HANDLE. I'LL GET THIS PLACE SHIPSHAPE IN THE MEANTIME.
I TRUST YOU FOUND YOUR PAGERS?
WHY... OF COURSE WE DID, SIR.
GOOD! KEEP THEM HANDY IN CASE I NEED TO CONTACT YOU.

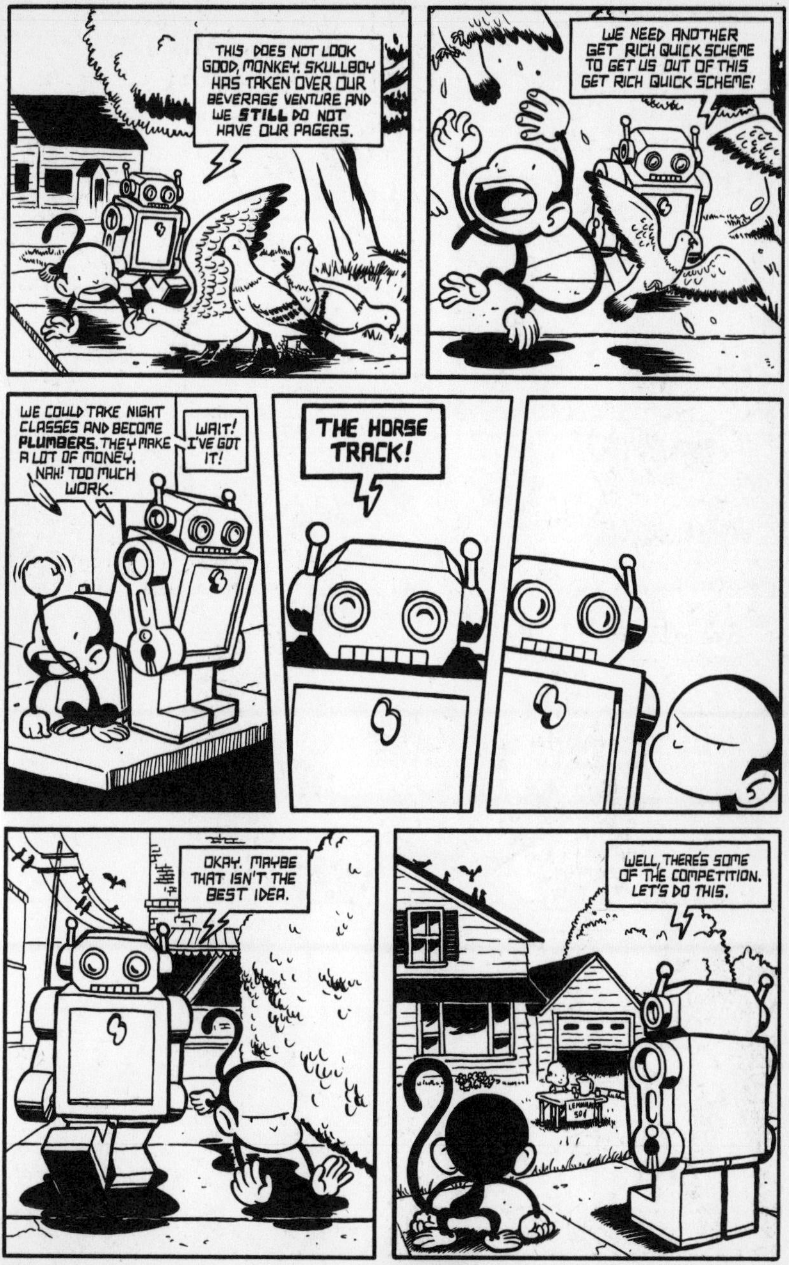
THIS DOES NOT LOOK GOOD, MONKEY. SKULLBOY HAS TAKEN OVER OUR BEVERAGE VENTURE AND WE STILL DO NOT HAVE OUR PAGERS.
WE NEED ANOTHER GET RICH QUICK SCHEME TO GET US OUT OF THIS GET RICH QUICK SCHEME!
WE COULD TAKE NIGHT CLASSES AND BECOME PLUMBERS. THEY MAKE A LOT OF MONEY.
NAH! TOO MUCH WORK.
WAIT! I'VE GOT IT!
THE HORSE TRACK!
OKAY. MAYBE THAT ISN'T THE BEST IDEA.
WELL, THERE'S SOME OF THE COMPETITION. LET'S DO THIS.

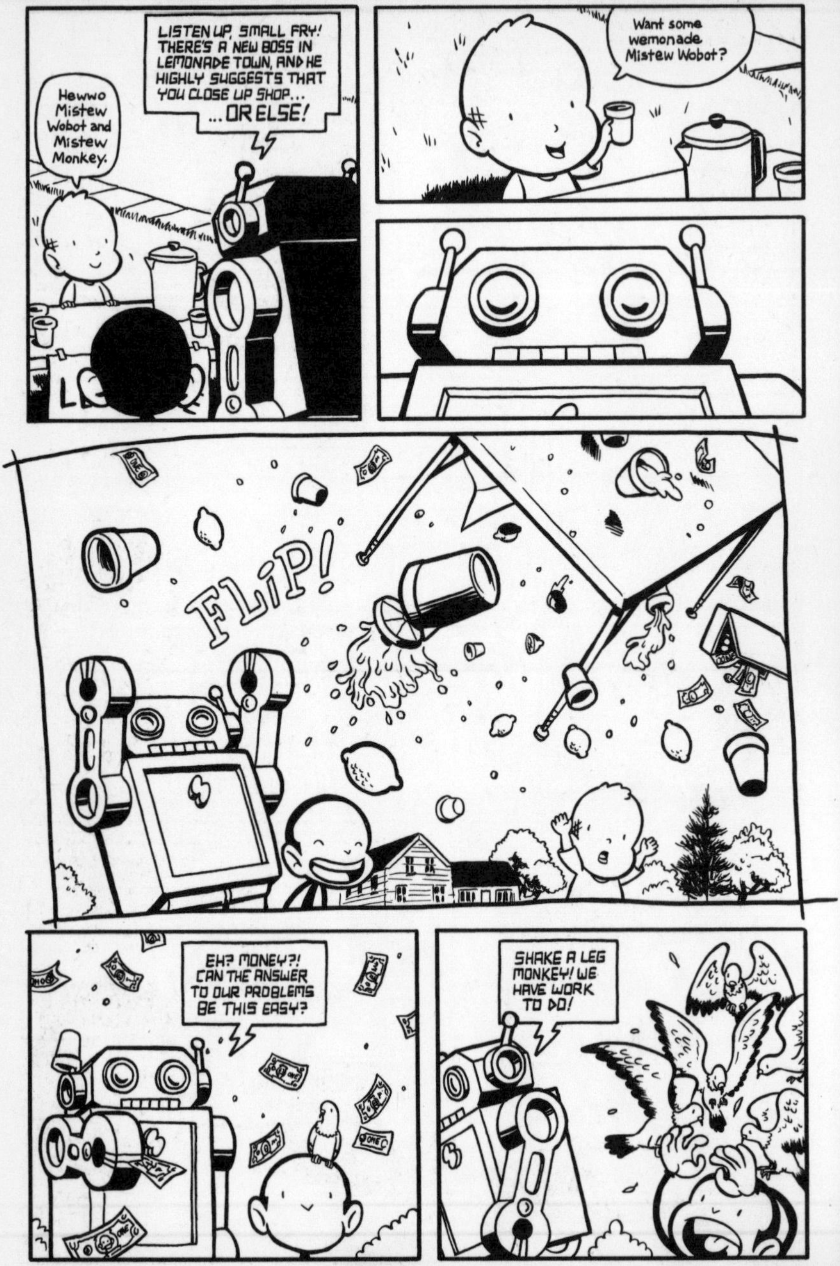
Hewwo Mistew Wobot and Mistew Monkey.
LISTEN UP, SMALL FRY! THERE'S A NEW BOSS IN LEMONADE TOWN, AND HE HIGHLY SUGGESTS THAT YOU CLOSE UP SHOP... ...OR ELSE!
Want some wemonade Mistew Wobot?
FLIP!
EH? MONEY?! CAN THE ANSWER TO OUR PROBLEMS BE THIS EASY?
SHAKE A LEG MONKEY! WE HAVE WORK TO DO!

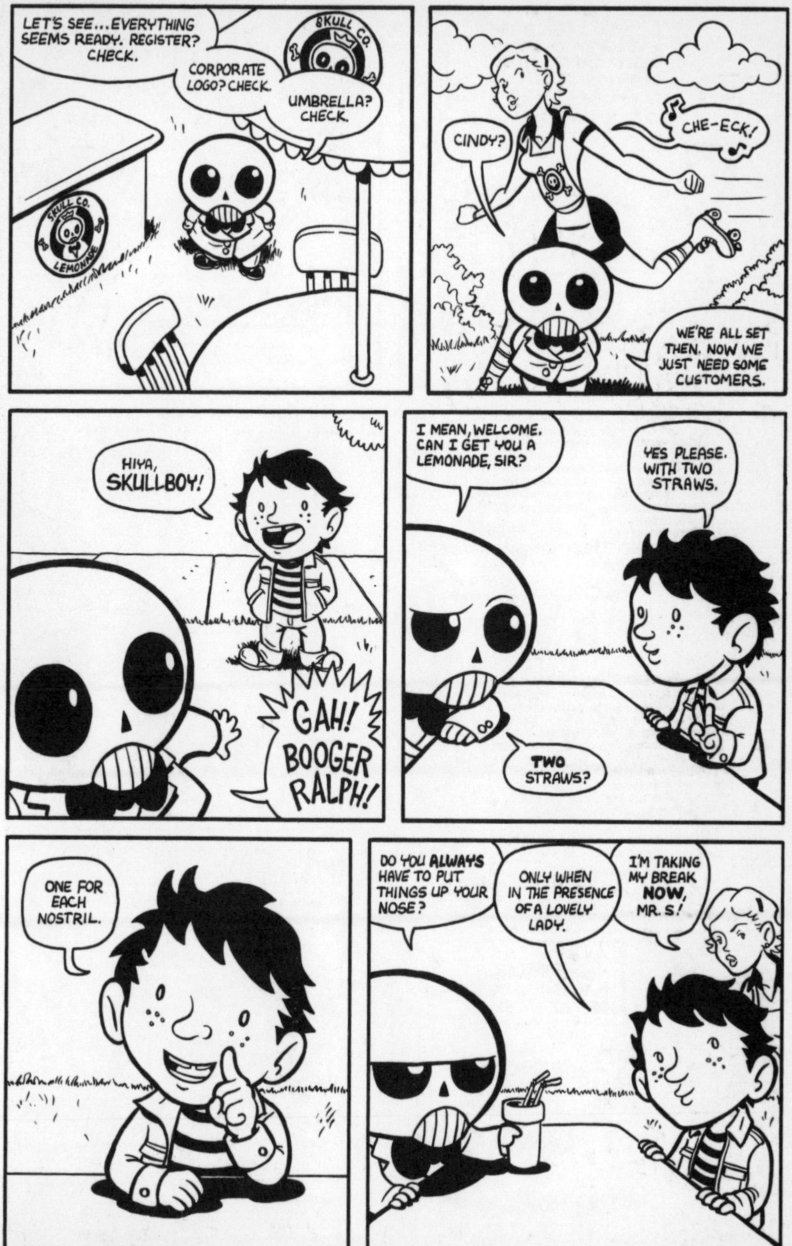
LET'S SEE...EVERYTHING SEEMS READY. REGISTER? CHECK.
SKULL CO.
CORPORATE LOGO? CHECK.
UMBRELLA? CHECK.
SKULL CO. LEMONADE
CINDY?
CHE-ECK!
WE'RE ALL SET THEN. NOW WE JUST NEED SOME CUSTOMERS.
HIYA, SKULLBOY!
GAH! BOOGER RALPH!
I MEAN, WELCOME. CAN I GET YOU A LEMONADE, SIR?
YES PLEASE. WITH TWO STRAWS.
TWO STRAWS?
ONE FOR EACH NOSTRIL.
DO YOU ALWAYS HAVE TO PUT THINGS UP YOUR NOSE?
ONLY WHEN IN THE PRESENCE OF A LOVELY LADY.
I'M TAKING MY BREAK NOW, MR. S!

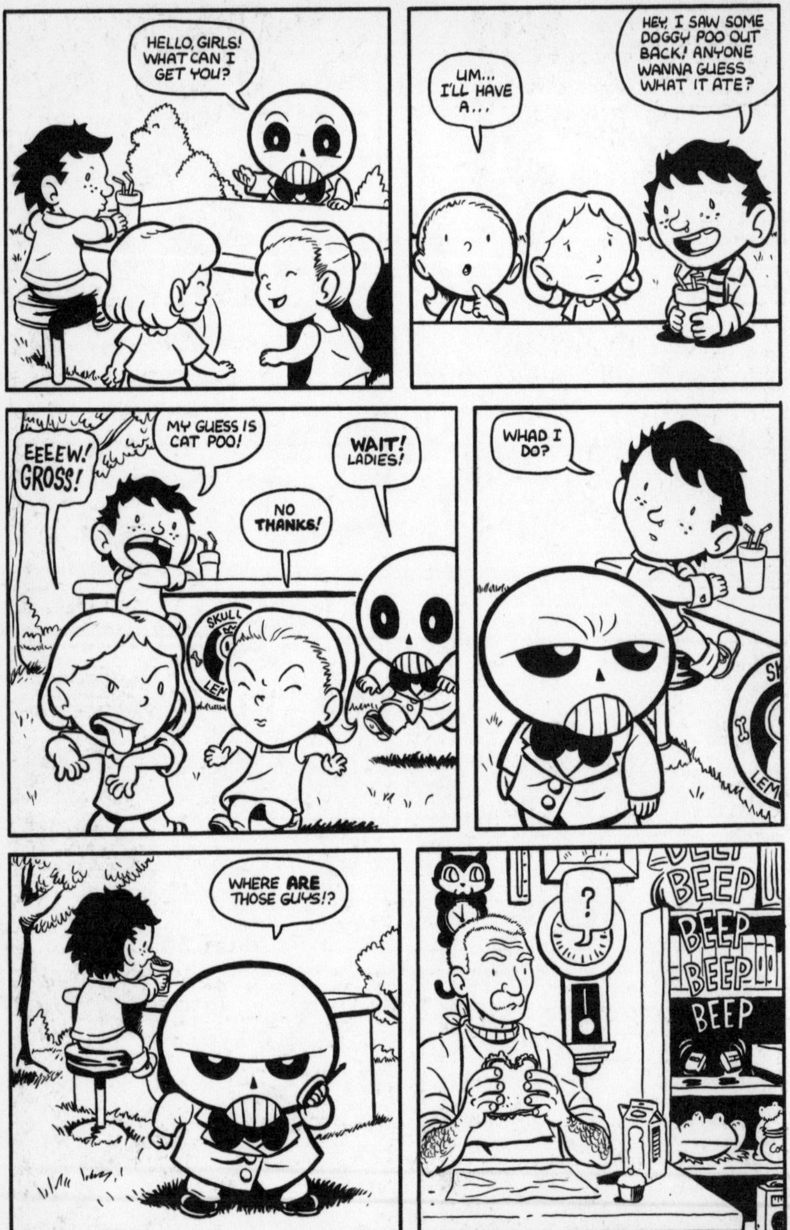
HELLO, GIRLS! WHAT CAN I GET YOU?
UM... I'LL HAVE A...
HEY, I SAW SOME DOGGY POO OUT BACK! ANYONE WANNA GUESS WHAT IT ATE?
EEEEW! GROSS!
MY GUESS IS CAT POO!
NO THANKS!
WAIT! LADIES!
SKULL
LEM
WHAD I DO?
WHERE ARE THOSE GUYS!?
?
BEEP
BEEP
BEEP
BEEP

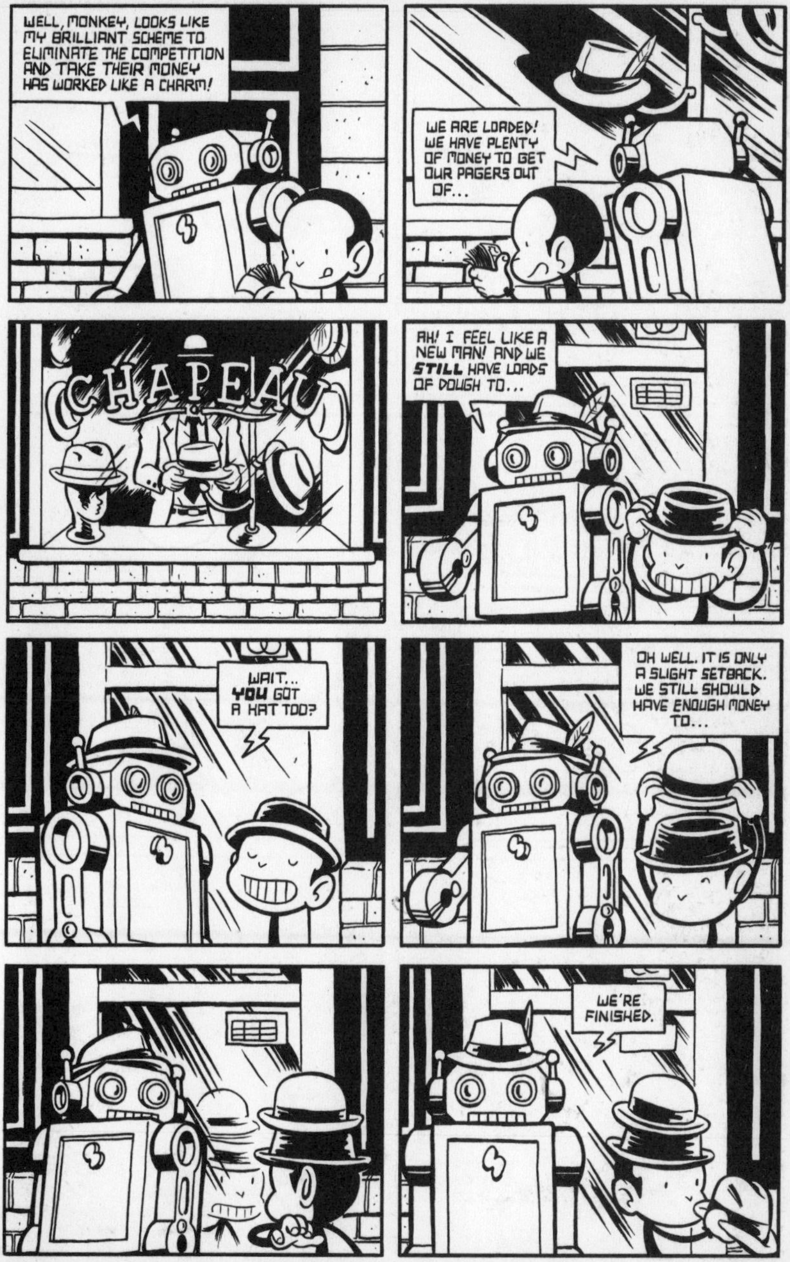
WELL, MONKEY, LOOKS LIKE MY BRILLIANT SCHEME TO ELIMINATE THE COMPETITION AND TAKE THEIR MONEY HAS WORKED LIKE A CHARM!
WE ARE LOADED! WE HAVE PLENTY OF MONEY TO GET OUR PAGERS OUT OF...
CHAPEAU
AH! I FEEL LIKE A NEW MAN! AND WE STILL HAVE LOADS OF DOUGH TO...
WAIT... YOU GOT A HAT TOO?
OH WELL. IT IS ONLY A SLIGHT SETBACK. WE STILL SHOULD HAVE ENOUGH MONEY TO...
WE'RE FINISHED.

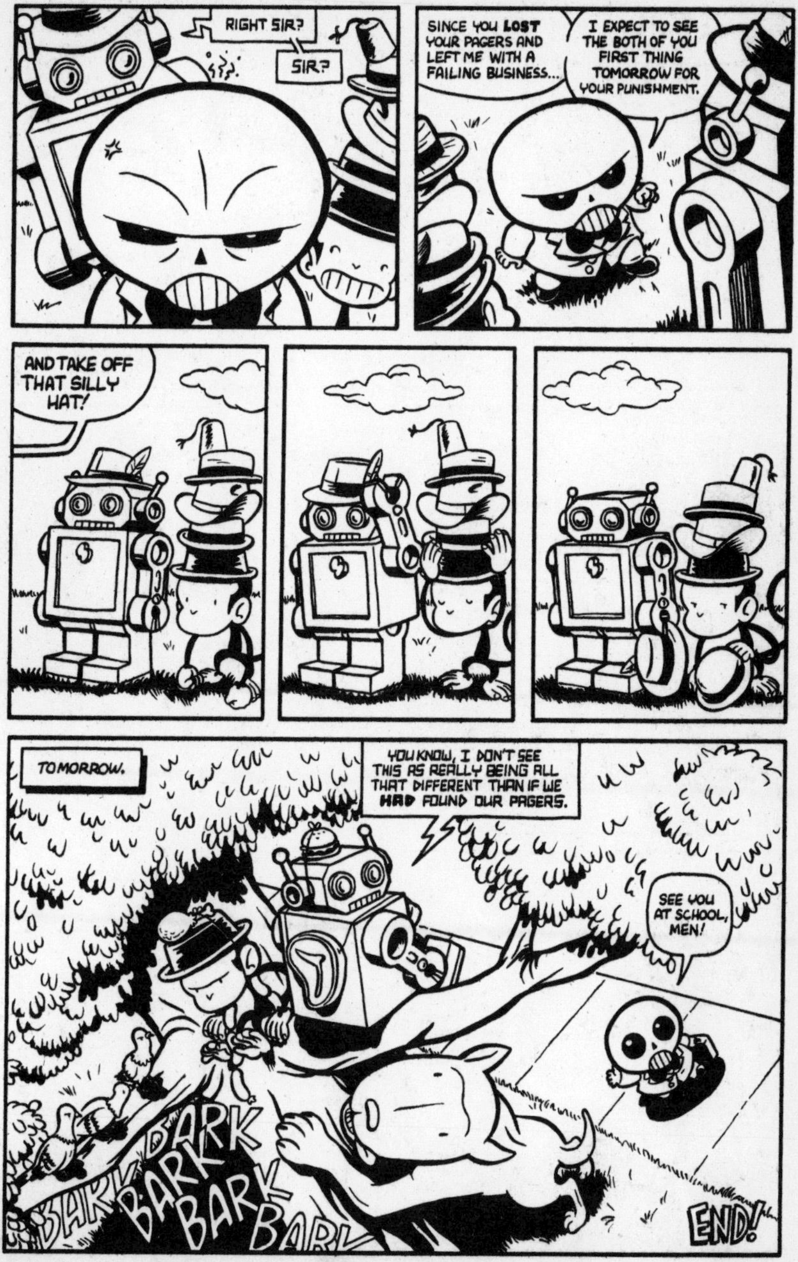
RIGHT SIR?
SIR?
SINCE YOU LOST YOUR PAGERS AND LEFT ME WITH A FAILING BUSINESS...
I EXPECT TO SEE THE BOTH OF YOU FIRST THING TOMORROW FOR YOUR PUNISHMENT.
AND TAKE OFF THAT SILLY HAT!
TOMORROW.
YOU KNOW, I DON'T SEE THIS AS REALLY BEING ALL THAT DIFFERENT THAN IF WE HAD FOUND OUR PAGERS.
SEE YOU AT SCHOOL, MEN!
BARK BARK BARK BARK BARK BARK
END!

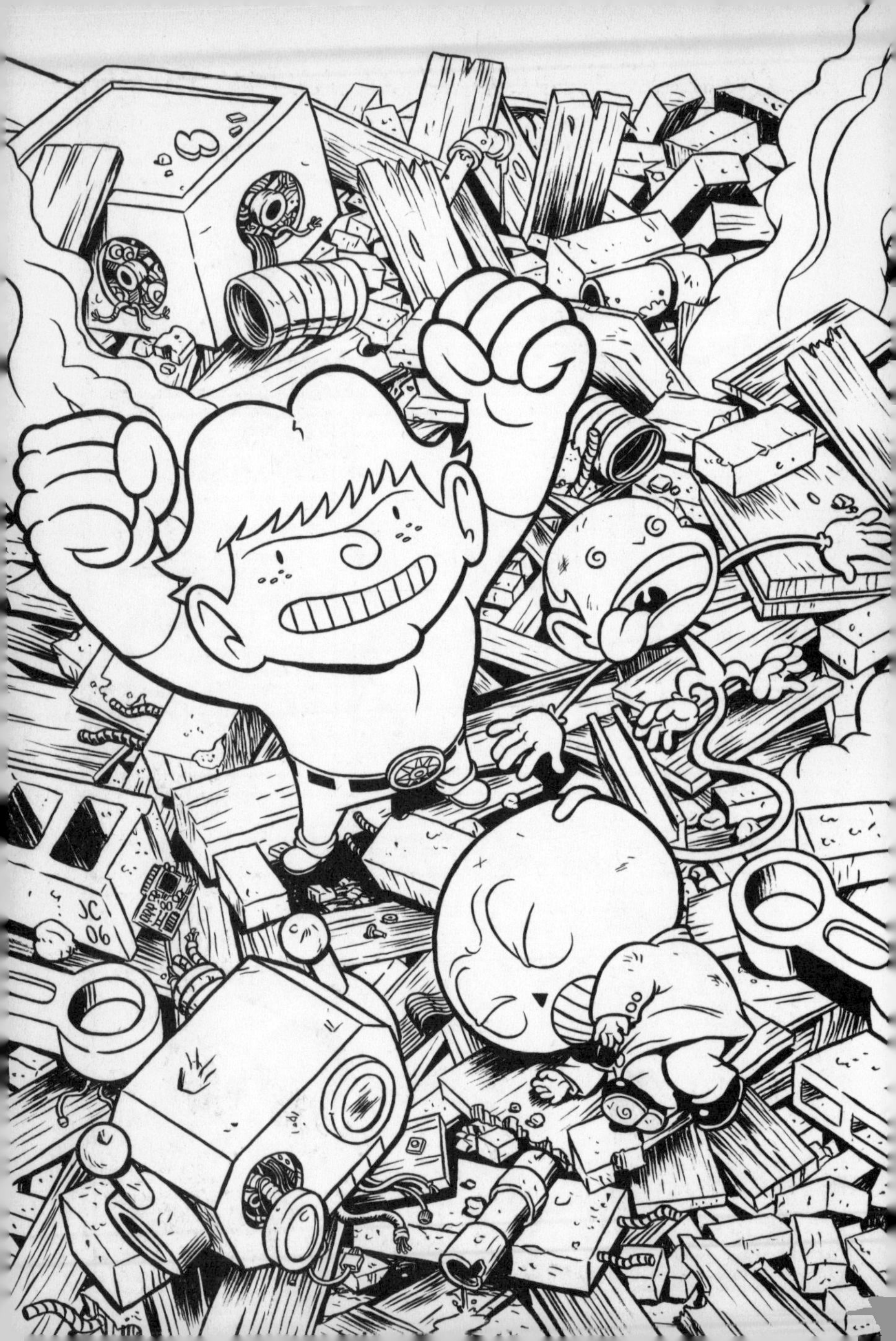
JC
06

A MiGHTY SKULLBOY ARMY ROMP!

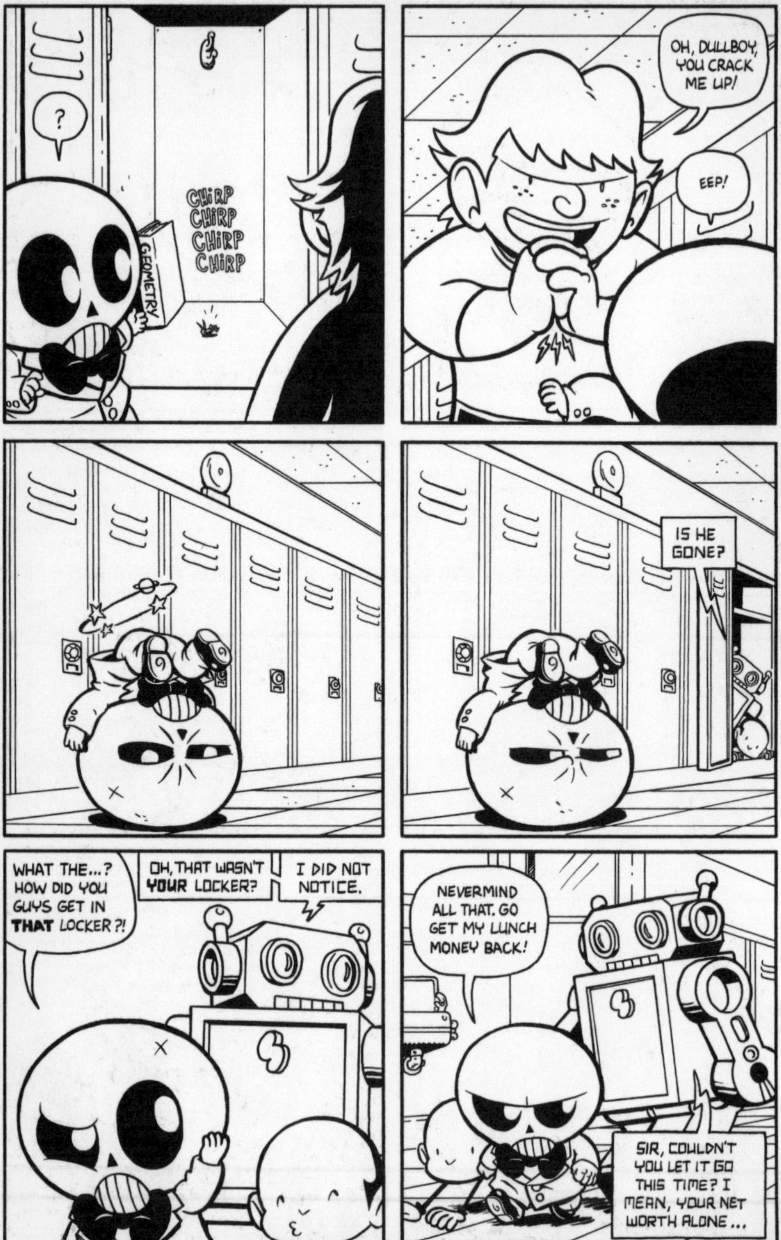
?
GEOMETRY
CHIRP CHIRP CHIRP CHIRP
OH, DULLBOY, YOU CRACK ME UP!
EEP!
IS HE GONE?
WHAT THE...? HOW DID YOU GUYS GET IN THAT LOCKER?!
OH, THAT WASN'T YOUR LOCKER?
I DID NOT NOTICE.
NEVERMIND ALL THAT. GO GET MY LUNCH MONEY BACK!
SIR, COULDN'T YOU LET IT GO THIS TIME? I MEAN, YOUR NET WORTH ALONE...

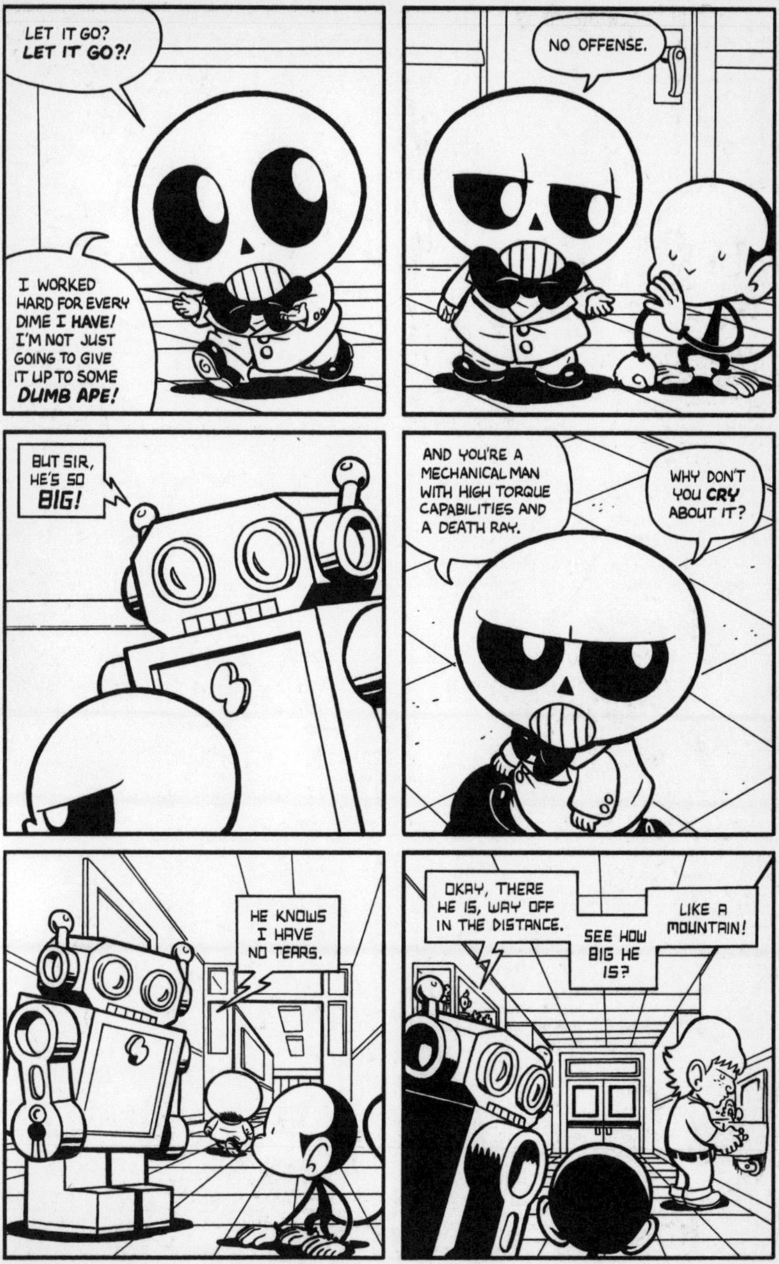
LET IT GO? LET IT GO?!
I WORKED HARD FOR EVERY DIME I HAVE! I'M NOT JUST GOING TO GIVE IT UP TO SOME DUMB APE!
NO OFFENSE.
BUT SIR, HE'S SO BIG!
AND YOU'RE A MECHANICAL MAN WITH HIGH TORQUE CAPABILITIES AND A DEATH RAY.
WHY DON'T YOU CRY ABOUT IT?
HE KNOWS I HAVE NO TEARS.
OKAY, THERE HE IS, WAY OFF IN THE DISTANCE.
SEE HOW BIG HE IS?
LIKE A MOUNTAIN!

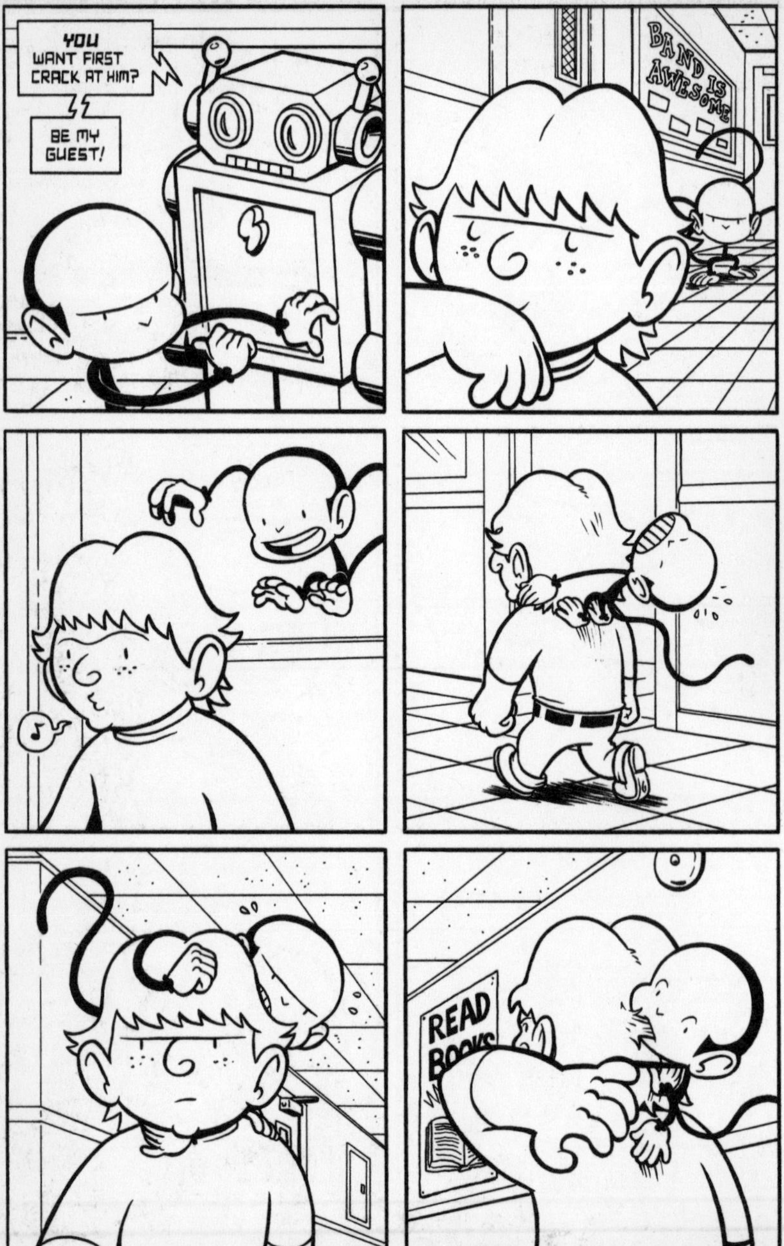
YOU WANT FIRST CRACK AT HIM?
BE MY GUEST!
BAND IS AWESOME
READ BOOKS

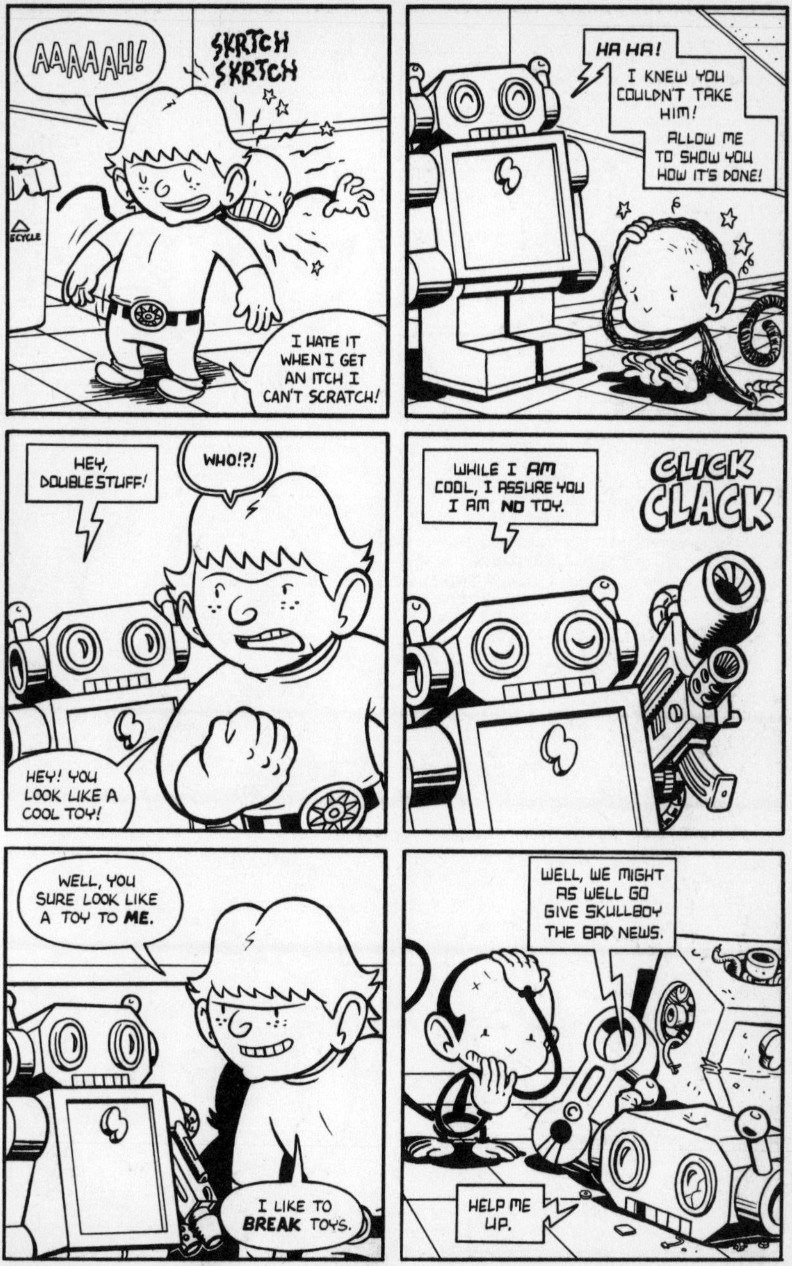
AAAAAH!
SKRTCH SKRTCH
I HATE IT WHEN I GET AN ITCH I CAN'T SCRATCH!
HA HA!
I KNEW YOU COULDN'T TAKE HIM!
ALLOW ME TO SHOW YOU HOW IT'S DONE!
HEY, DOUBLESTUFF!
WHO!?!
HEY! YOU LOOK LIKE A COOL TOY!
WHILE I AM COOL, I ASSURE YOU I AM NO TOY.
CLICK CLACK
WELL, YOU SURE LOOK LIKE A TOY TO ME.
I LIKE TO BREAK TOYS.
WELL, WE MIGHT AS WELL GO GIVE SKULLBOY THE BAD NEWS.
HELP ME UP.

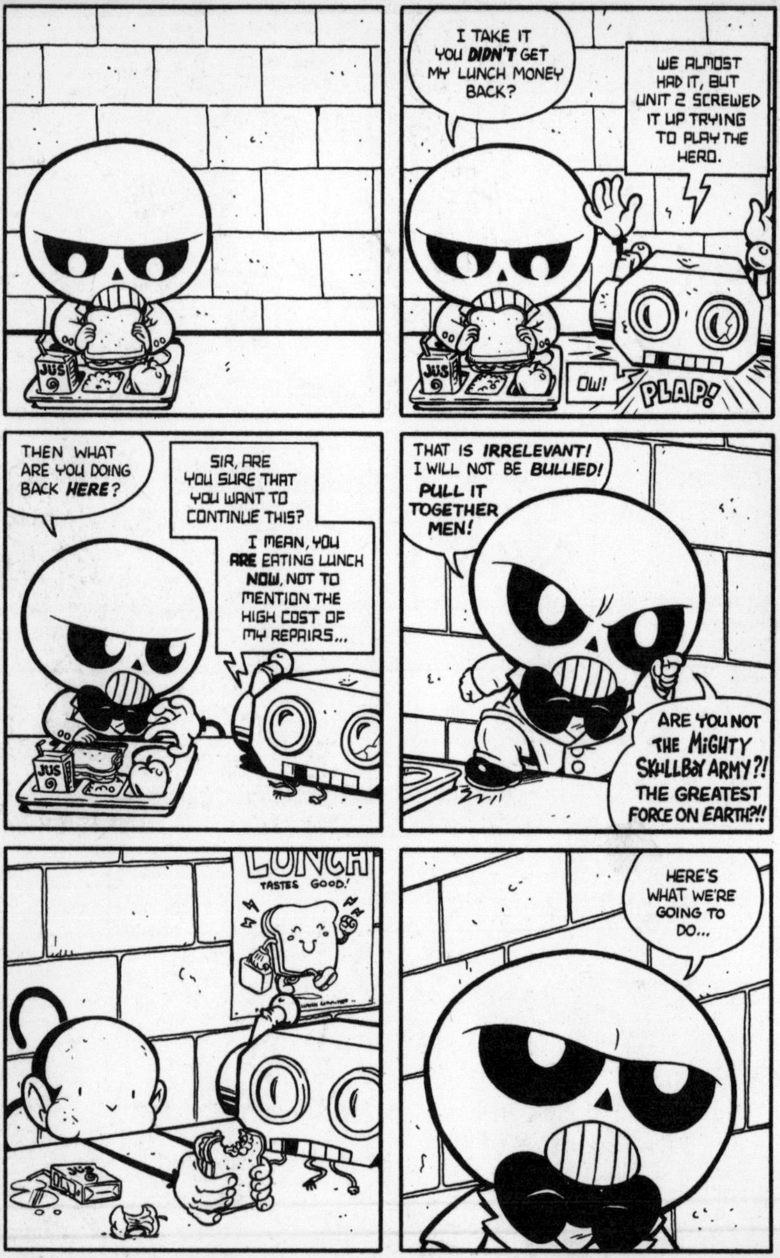
I TAKE IT YOU DIDN'T GET MY LUNCH MONEY BACK?
WE ALMOST HAD IT, BUT UNIT 2 SCREWED IT UP TRYING TO PLAY THE HERO.
JUS
OW!
PLAP!
THEN WHAT ARE YOU DOING BACK HERE?
SIR, ARE YOU SURE THAT YOU WANT TO CONTINUE THIS?
I MEAN, YOU ARE EATING LUNCH NOW, NOT TO MENTION THE HIGH COST OF MY REPAIRS...
THAT IS IRRELEVANT! I WILL NOT BE BULLIED! PULL IT TOGETHER MEN!
ARE YOU NOT THE MIGHTY SKULLBOY ARMY?! THE GREATEST FORCE ON EARTH?!!
LUNCH
TASTES GOOD!
HERE'S WHAT WE'RE GOING TO DO...

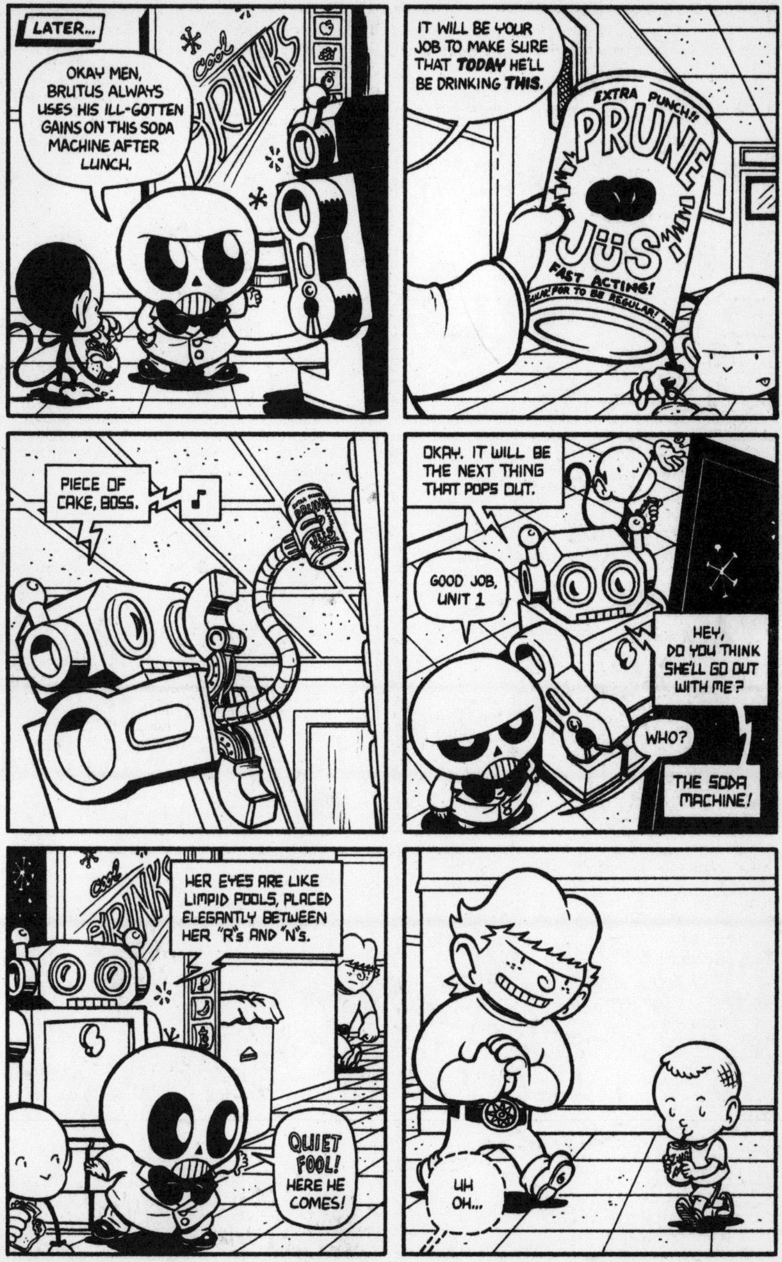
LATER...
OKAY MEN, BRUTUS ALWAYS USES HIS ILL-GOTTEN GAINS ON THIS SODA MACHINE AFTER LUNCH.
cool DRINKS
IT WILL BE YOUR JOB TO MAKE SURE THAT **TODAY** HE'LL BE DRINKING **THIS.**
EXTRA PUNCH!!
PRUNE
JüS
FAST ACTING!
FOR TO BE REGULAR!
PIECE OF CAKE, BOSS.
OKAY. IT WILL BE THE NEXT THING THAT POPS OUT.
GOOD JOB, UNIT 1
HEY, DO YOU THINK SHE'LL GO OUT WITH ME?
WHO?
THE SODA MACHINE!
HER EYES ARE LIKE LIMPID POOLS, PLACED ELEGANTLY BETWEEN HER "R"s AND "N"s.
QUIET FOOL! HERE HE COMES!
UH OH...

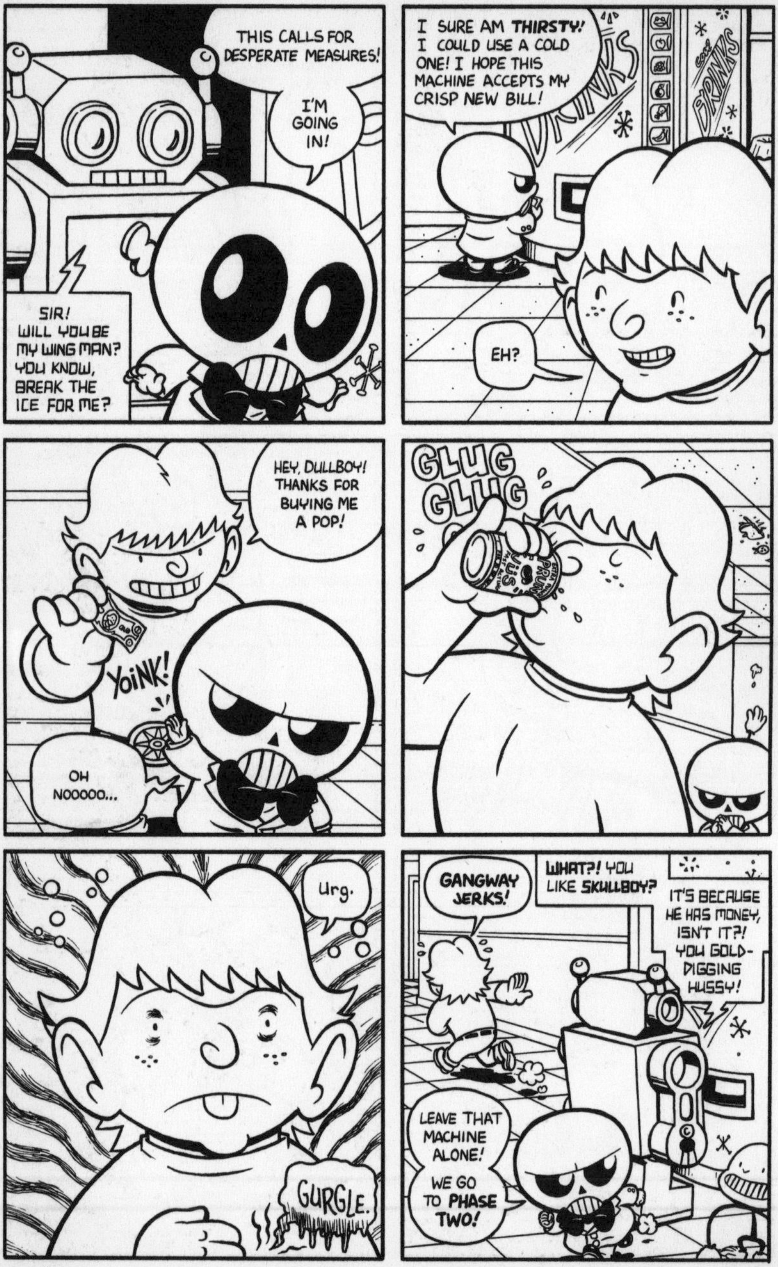
THIS CALLS FOR DESPERATE MEASURES!
I'M GOING IN!
SIR! WILL YOU BE MY WING MAN? YOU KNOW, BREAK THE ICE FOR ME?
I SURE AM THIRSTY! I COULD USE A COLD ONE! I HOPE THIS MACHINE ACCEPTS MY CRISP NEW BILL!
DRINKS
COOL DRINKS
EH?
HEY, DULLBOY! THANKS FOR BUYING ME A POP!
YOINK!
OH NOOOOO...
GLUG GLUG
PRUNE JUS
Urg.
GURGLE.
GANGWAY JERKS!
WHAT?! YOU LIKE SKULLBOY?
IT'S BECAUSE HE HAS MONEY, ISN'T IT?! YOU GOLD-DIGGING HUSSY!
LEAVE THAT MACHINE ALONE!
WE GO TO PHASE TWO!

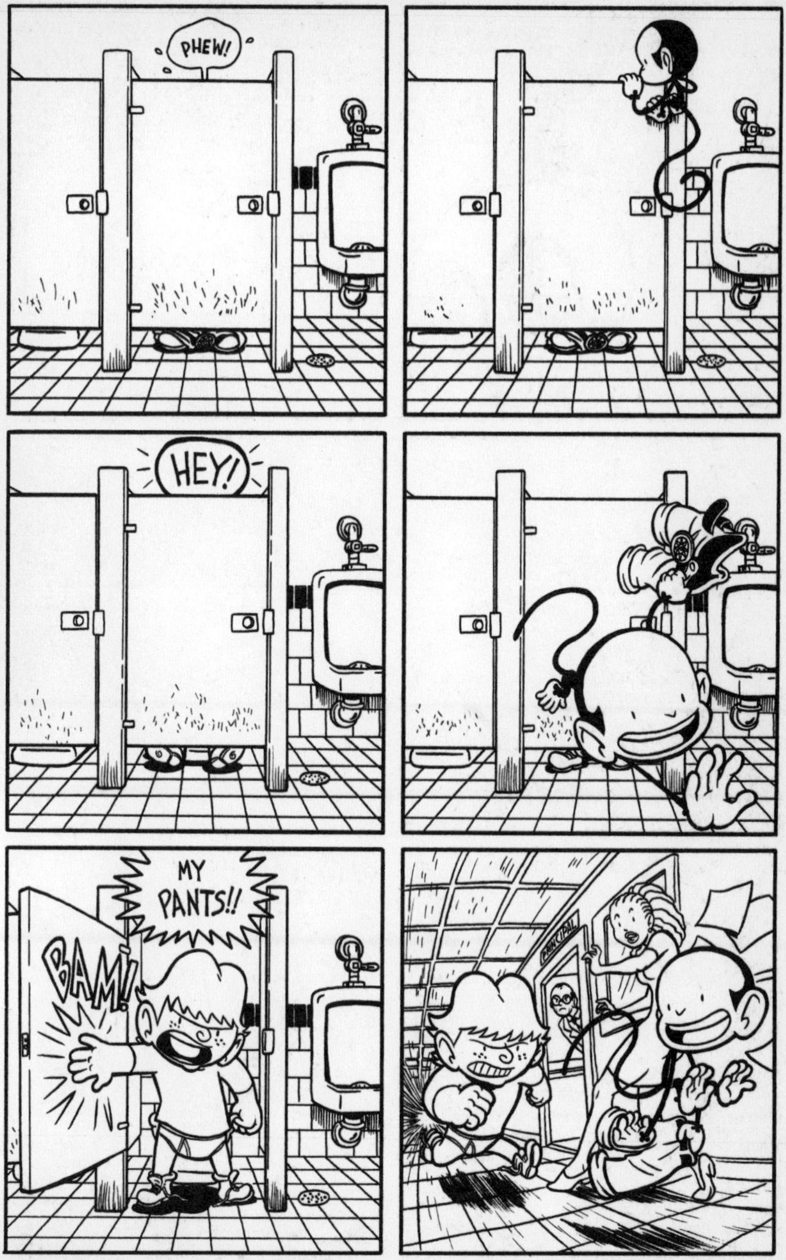
PHEW!
HEY!
MY PANTS!!
BAM!
PRINCIPAL

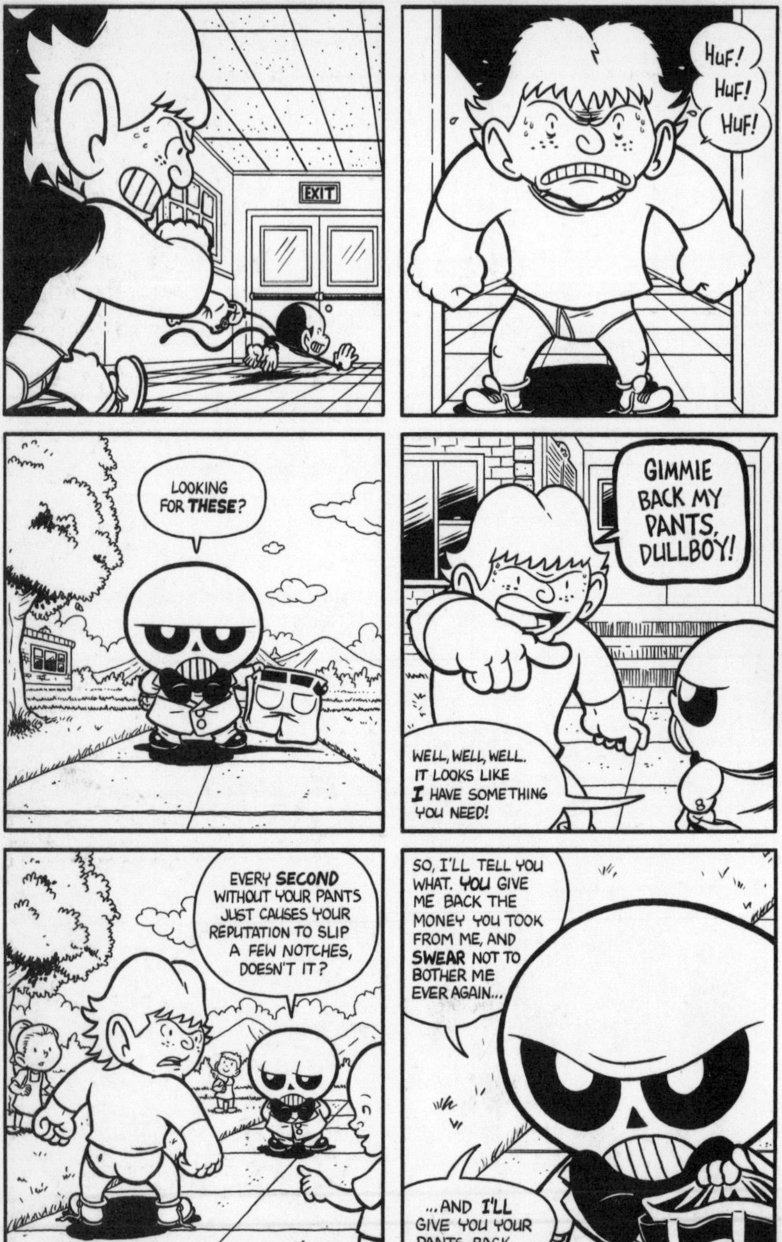
EXIT
HUF!
HUF!
HUF!
LOOKING FOR THESE?
GIMMIE BACK MY PANTS, DULLBOY!
WELL, WELL, WELL. IT LOOKS LIKE I HAVE SOMETHING YOU NEED!
EVERY SECOND WITHOUT YOUR PANTS JUST CAUSES YOUR REPUTATION TO SLIP A FEW NOTCHES, DOESN'T IT?
SO, I'LL TELL YOU WHAT. YOU GIVE ME BACK THE MONEY YOU TOOK FROM ME, AND SWEAR NOT TO BOTHER ME EVER AGAIN...
...AND I'LL GIVE YOU YOUR PANTS BACK.

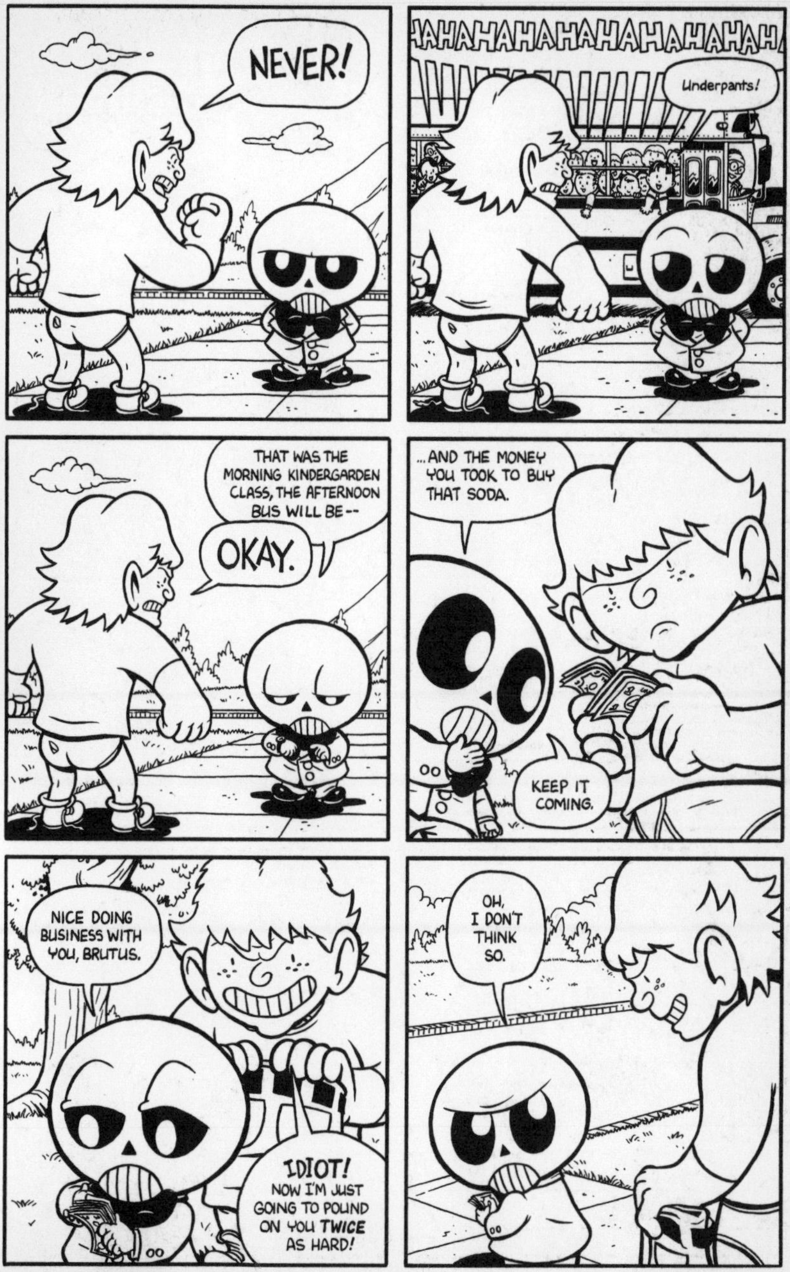
NEVER!
HAHAHAHAHAHAHAHAHAHAHAH
Underpants!
THAT WAS THE MORNING KINDERGARDEN CLASS, THE AFTERNOON BUS WILL BE--
OKAY.
...AND THE MONEY YOU TOOK TO BUY THAT SODA.
KEEP IT COMING.
NICE DOING BUSINESS WITH YOU, BRUTUS.
IDIOT! NOW I'M JUST GOING TO POUND ON YOU TWICE AS HARD!
OH, I DON'T THINK SO.

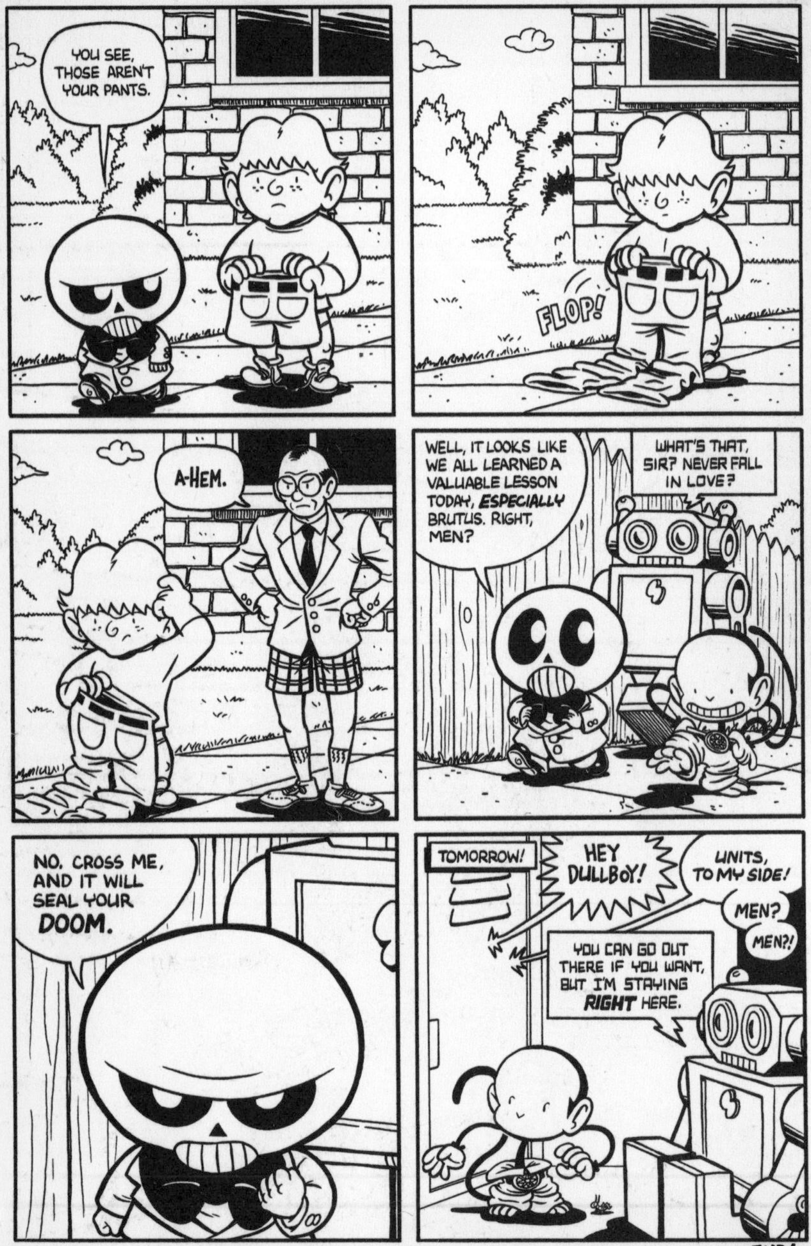
YOU SEE, THOSE AREN'T YOUR PANTS.
FLOP!
A-HEM.
WELL, IT LOOKS LIKE WE ALL LEARNED A VALUABLE LESSON TODAY, ESPECIALLY BRUTUS. RIGHT, MEN?
WHAT'S THAT, SIR? NEVER FALL IN LOVE?
NO. CROSS ME, AND IT WILL SEAL YOUR DOOM.
TOMORROW!
HEY DULLBOY!
UNITS, TO MY SIDE!
MEN?
MEN?!
YOU CAN GO OUT THERE IF YOU WANT, BUT I'M STAYING RIGHT HERE.
END!

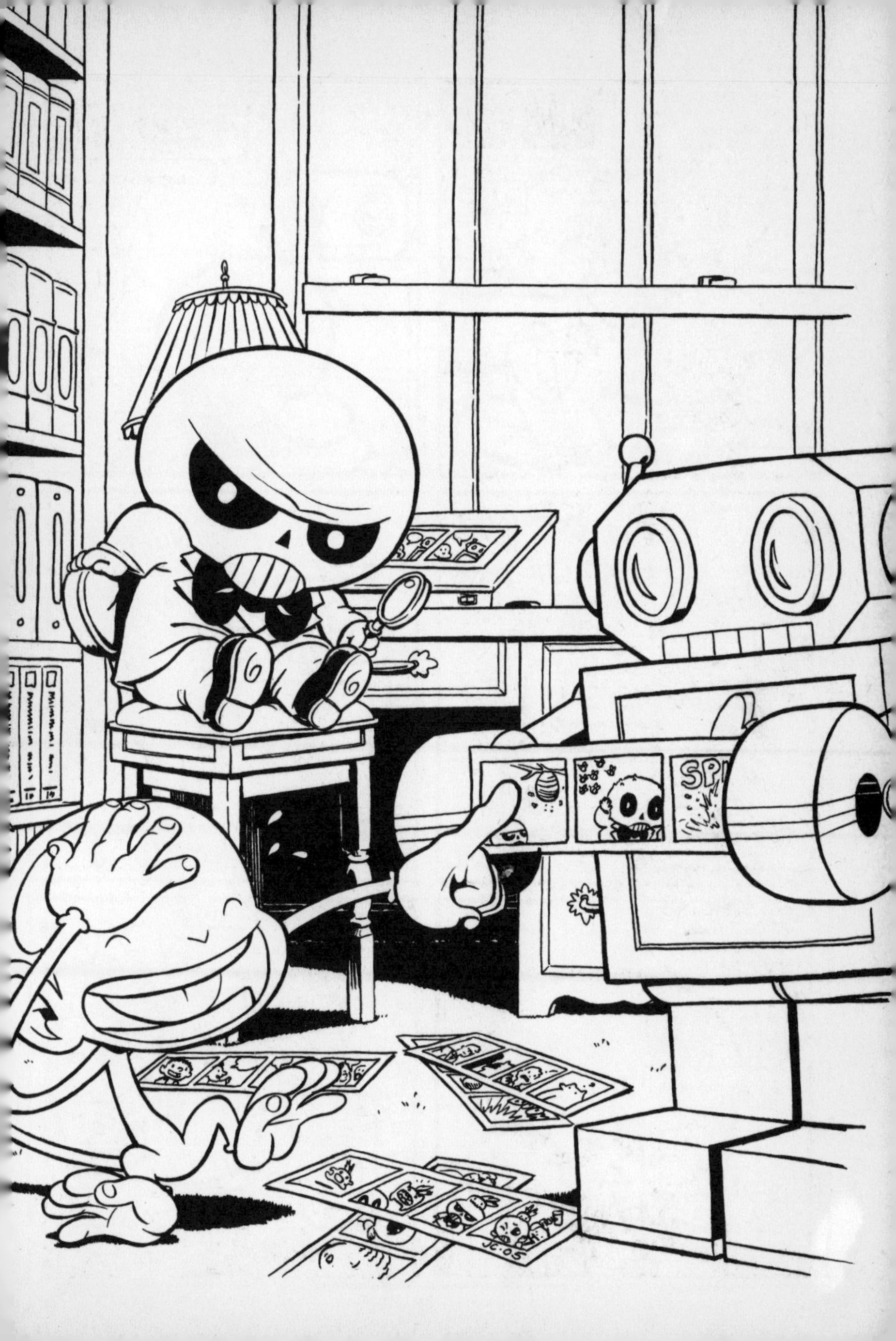
SP
JC·05

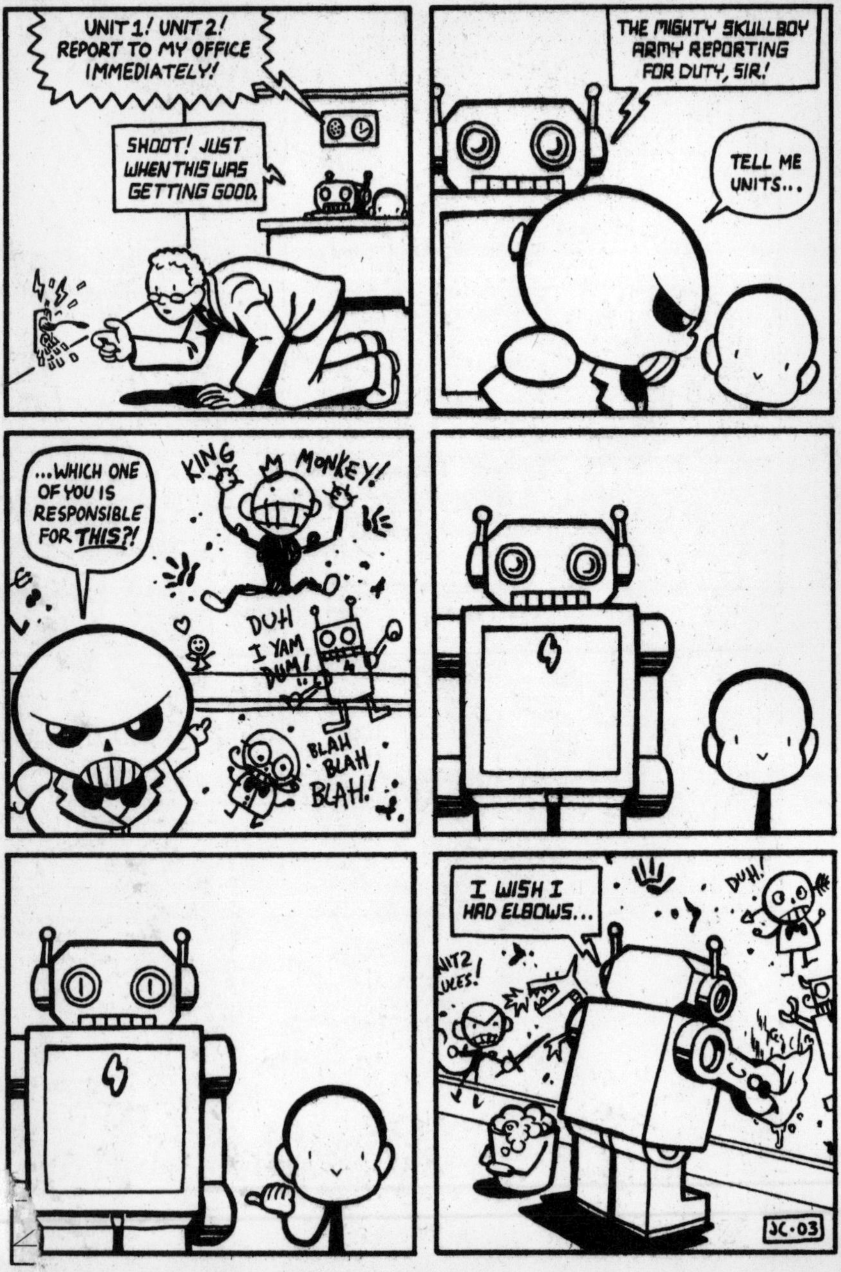

UNIT 1! UNIT 2! REPORT TO MY OFFICE IMMEDIATELY!
SHOOT! JUST WHEN THIS WAS GETTING GOOD.
THE MIGHTY SKULLBOY ARMY REPORTING FOR DUTY, SIR!
TELL ME UNITS...
...WHICH ONE OF YOU IS RESPONSIBLE FOR THIS?!
KING MONKEY!
DUH I YAM DUM!
BLAH BLAH BLAH!
I WISH I HAD ELBOWS...
DUH!
JC·03

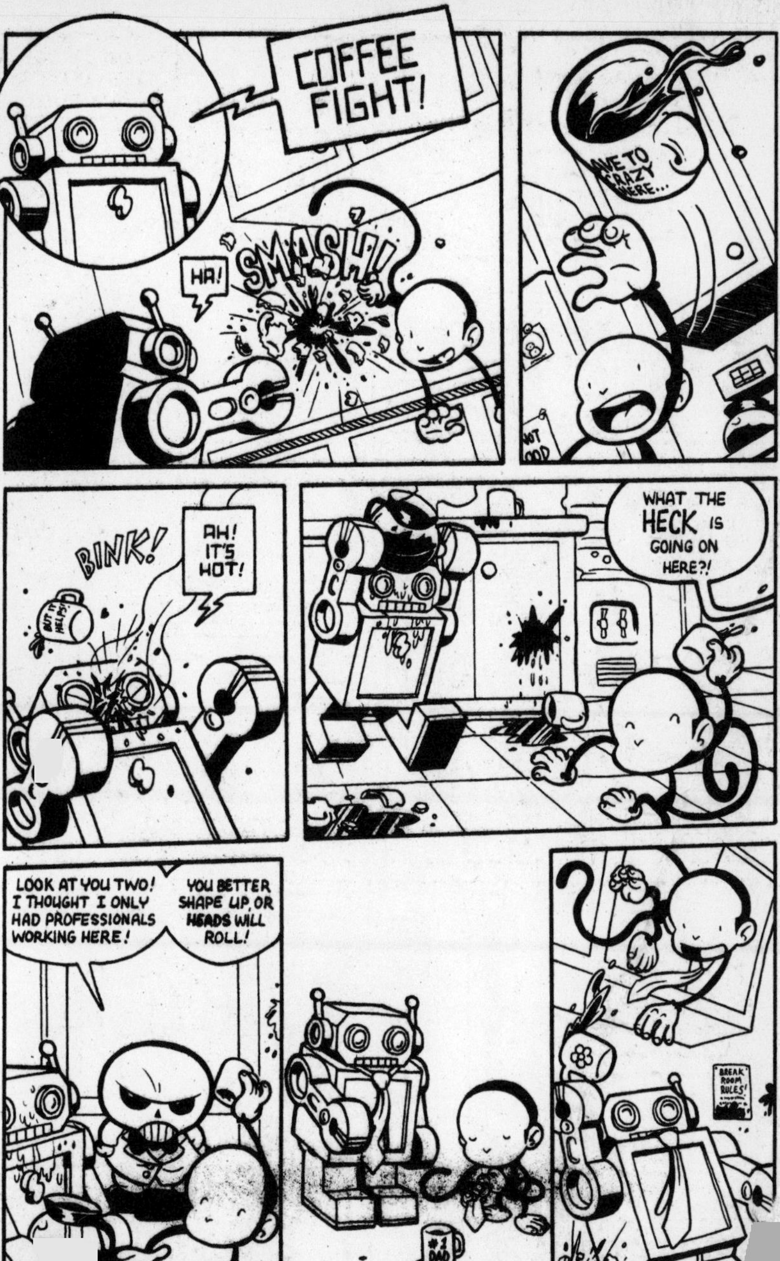
COFFEE FIGHT!
HA!
SMASH!
BINK!
BUT IT HELPS!
AH! IT'S HOT!
WHAT THE HECK IS GOING ON HERE?!
LOOK AT YOU TWO! I THOUGHT I ONLY HAD PROFESSIONALS WORKING HERE!
YOU BETTER SHAPE UP, OR HEADS WILL ROLL!
#1 DAD
BREAK ROOM RULES!

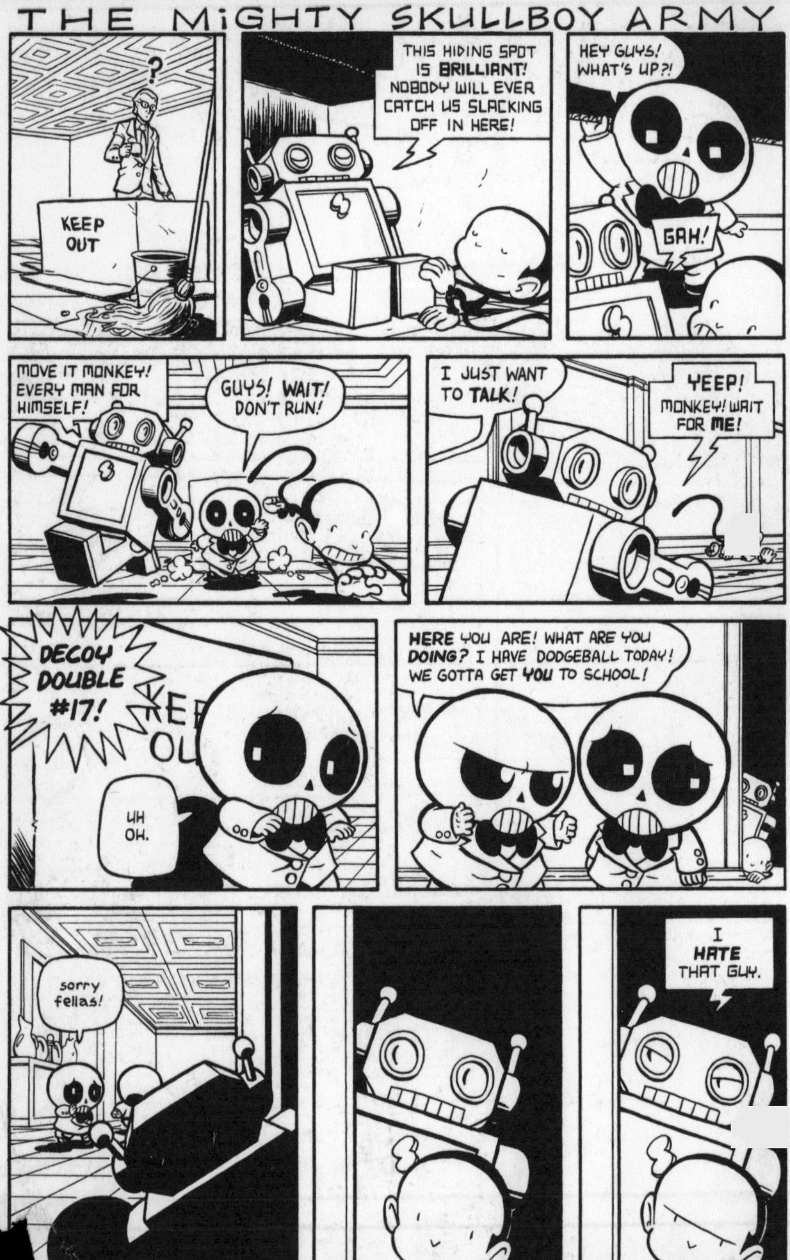
THE MIGHTY SKULLBOY ARMY
?
KEEP OUT
THIS HIDING SPOT IS BRILLIANT! NOBODY WILL EVER CATCH US SLACKING OFF IN HERE!
HEY GUYS! WHAT'S UP?!
GAH!
MOVE IT MONKEY! EVERY MAN FOR HIMSELF!
GUYS! WAIT! DON'T RUN!
I JUST WANT TO TALK!
YEEP! MONKEY! WAIT FOR ME!
DECOY DOUBLE #17!
UH OH.
HERE YOU ARE! WHAT ARE YOU DOING? I HAVE DODGEBALL TODAY! WE GOTTA GET YOU TO SCHOOL!
sorry fellas!
I HATE THAT GUY.
JACOB CHABOT 2005

The Mighty SKULLBOY ARMY

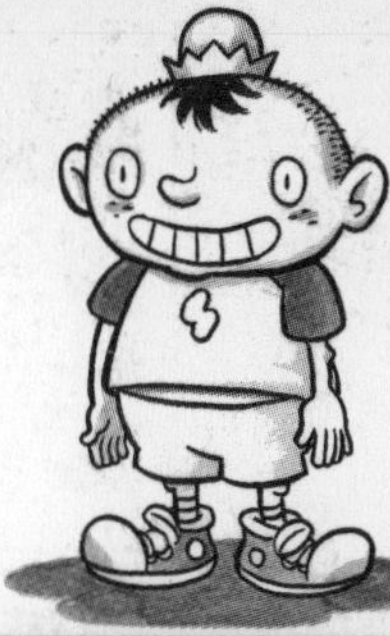

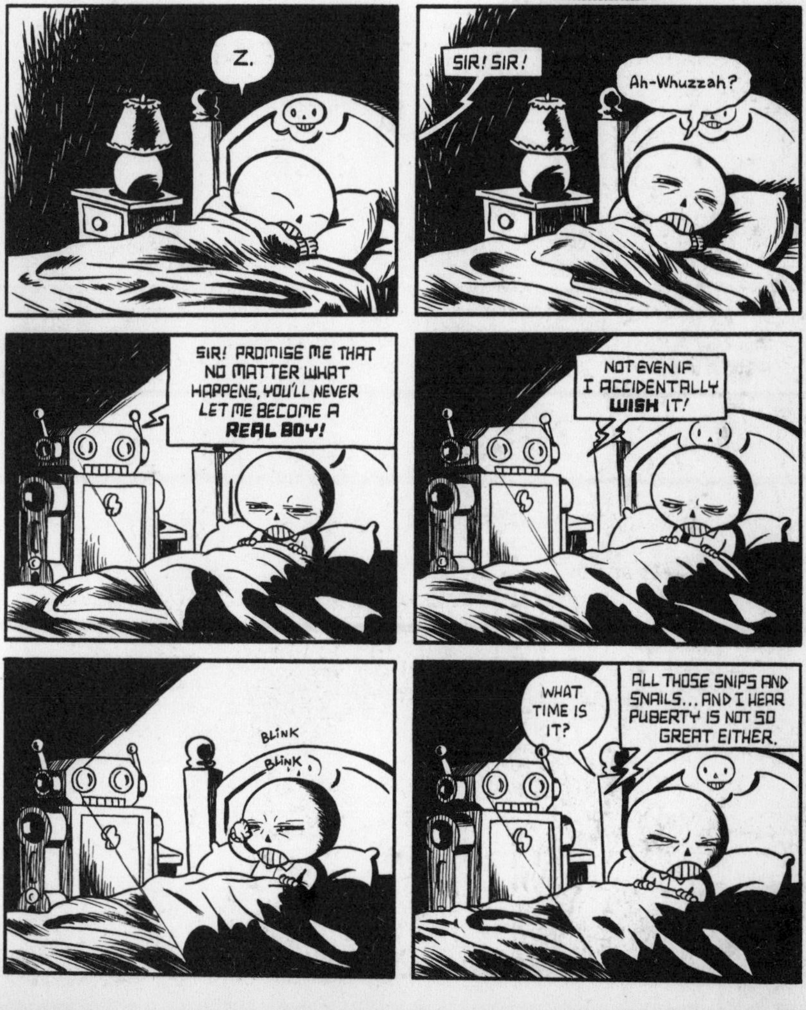

Z.
SIR! SIR!
Ah-Whuzzah?
SIR! PROMISE ME THAT NO MATTER WHAT HAPPENS, YOU'LL NEVER LET ME BECOME A REAL BOY!
NOT EVEN IF I ACCIDENTALLY WISH IT!
BLINK
BLINK
WHAT TIME IS IT?
ALL THOSE SNIPS AND SNAILS... AND I HEAR PUBERTY IS NOT SO GREAT EITHER.

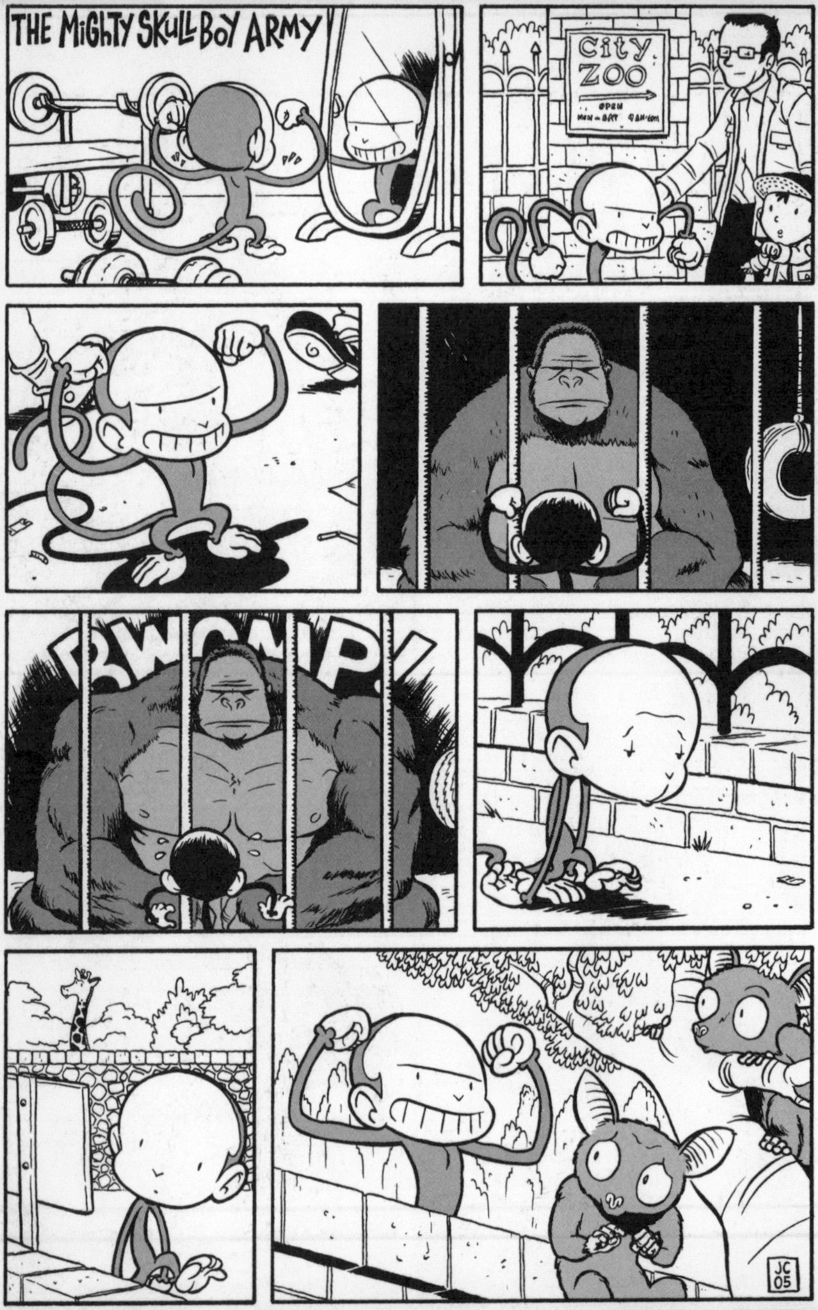
THE MIGHTY SKULLBOY ARMY
City ZOO
OPEN
BWOMP!
JC 05

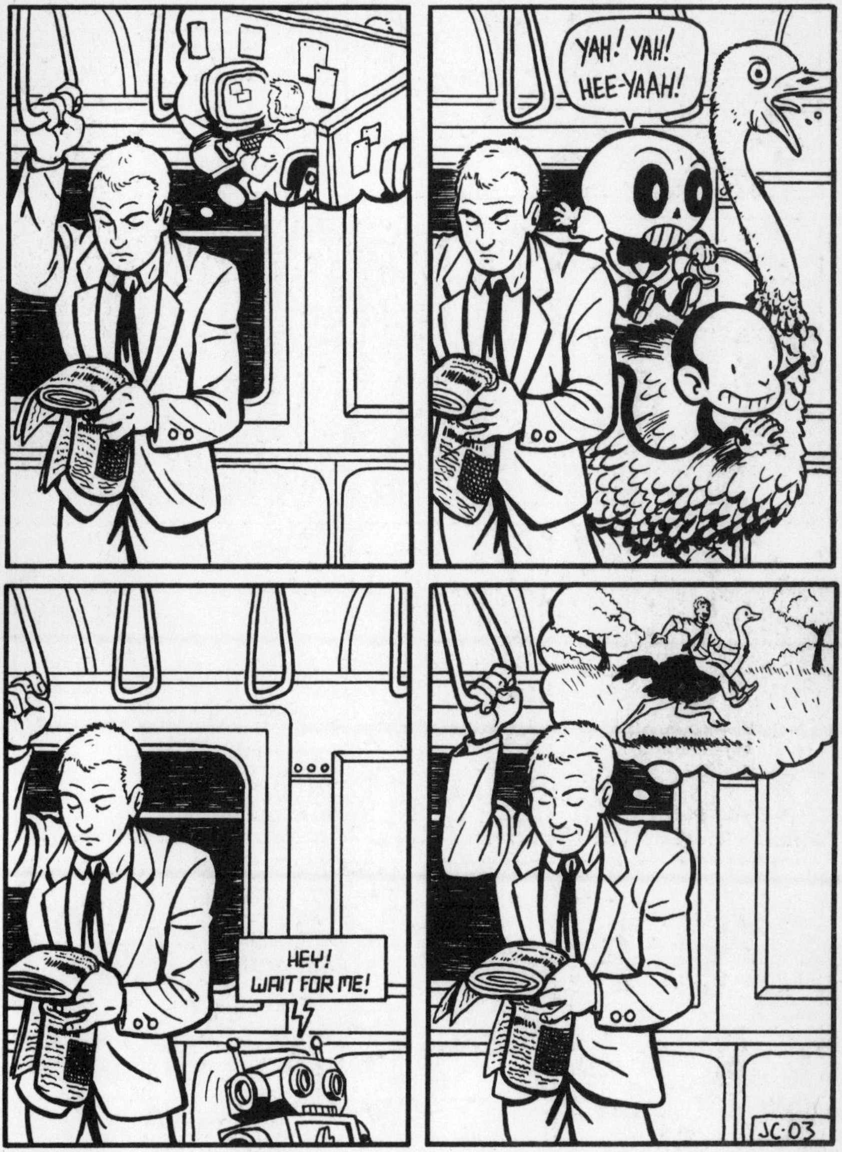
YAH! YAH!
HEE-YAAH!
HEY!
WAIT FOR ME!
JC·03

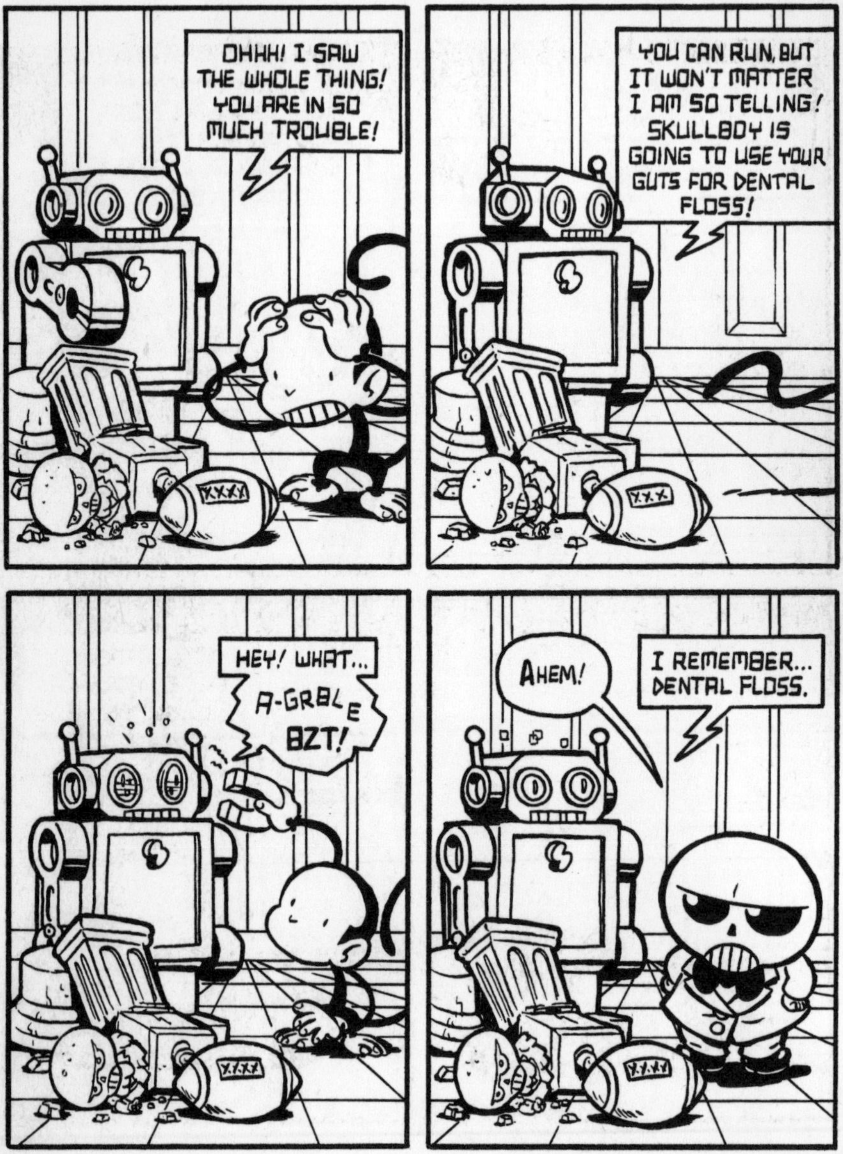
OHHH! I SAW THE WHOLE THING! YOU ARE IN SO MUCH TROUBLE!
YOU CAN RUN, BUT IT WON'T MATTER I AM SO TELLING! SKULLBOY IS GOING TO USE YOUR GUTS FOR DENTAL FLOSS!
HEY! WHAT...
A-GRBLE BZT!
AHEM!
I REMEMBER... DENTAL FLOSS.

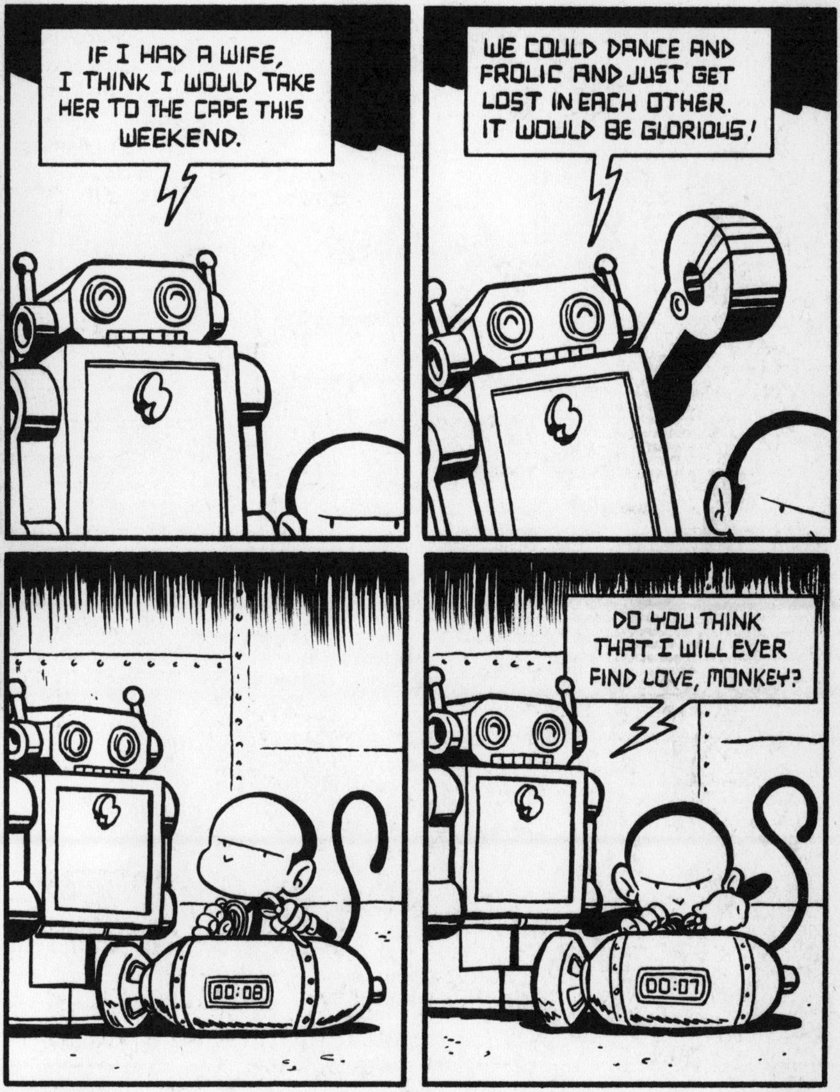
IF I HAD A WIFE, I THINK I WOULD TAKE HER TO THE CAPE THIS WEEKEND.
WE COULD DANCE AND FROLIC AND JUST GET LOST IN EACH OTHER. IT WOULD BE GLORIOUS!
00:08
DO YOU THINK THAT I WILL EVER FIND LOVE, MONKEY?
00:07

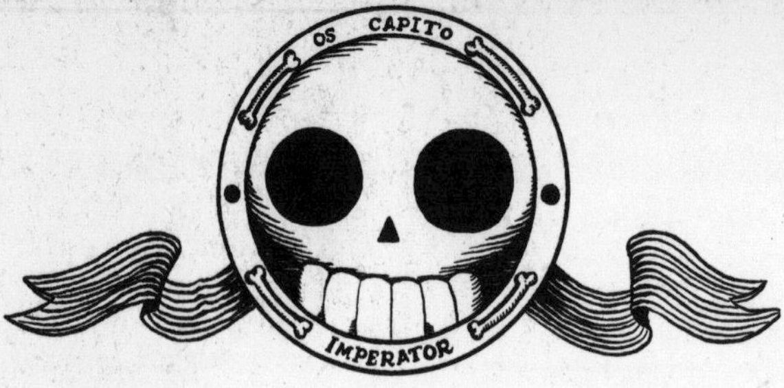
OS CAPITO
IMPERATOR

Publisher
Mike Richardson

Editor
Mike Carriglitto

Assistant Editors
Ryan Jorgensen & Samantha Robertson

Designer
Tony Ong

Art Director
Lia Ribacchi

Published by Dark Horse Books
a Division of
Dark Horse Comics, Inc.
10956 SE Main Street
Milwaukie, OR 97222
darkhorse.com

To find a comic shop in your area, call the Comic Shop Locator Service toll-free at 1-888-266-4226

First edition: February 2007

ISBN-10: 1-59307-629-0
ISBN-13: 978-1-59307-629-0

1 3 5 7 9 10 8 6 4 2
Printed in Canada